FROM NETWORKS TO SMART DEVICES: UNDERSTANDING IOT

Ms. Vandana Dabass
Ms. Neerja
Dr. Meenu
Dr. Madhu Chauhan

TANEESHA PUBLISHING

ISBN : 9788199862562
Edition : First, March 2026
Title : From Networks to Smart Devices: Understanding IoT
Author : Ms. Vandana Dabass, Ms. Neerja, Dr. Meenu, Dr. Madhu Chauhan

Published by

TANEESHA PUBLISHING

An Imprint of **Taneesha and Prachi NextGen Publication**

Registered Office: Sunil Complex, 2nd Floor, Vijay Nagar,
Western Kutchery Road, Meerut - 250002, Uttar Pradesh, India
Website : www.taneeshapublishing.com
E-mail : support@tpnextpub.com
Phone : +91 9760418103

Printed by :
Manipal Technologies Limited, Bengaluru - 560001, Karnataka

INDEX – IoT (Internet of Things)

Unit-1

Basics of Networking

1.1 Introduction to Computer Networks

A computer network is a system in which multiple digital devices are linked together to communicate and exchange information. It connects equipment such as computers, servers, printers, and various other electronic tools. By sharing resources and data among these devices, networks make it possible to perform tasks like browsing the internet, sending emails, transferring files, and using shared software efficiently.

Basic Terminologies of Computer Networks

Basic computer network terms include **network** (a collection of interconnected devices), **node** (any device on a network), **protocol** (a set of rules for communication), **IP address** (a unique numerical identifier for a device), and **router** (a device that forwards data between networks). Other key terms are **LAN** (Local Area Network for a small area) and **WAN** (Wide Area Network for a large area).

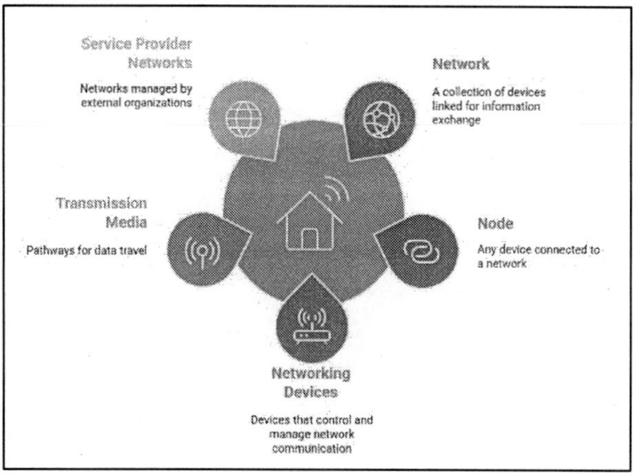

Fig. 1.1 Components of Computer Networks

- **Network**: A network refers to a collection of devices linked together so they can exchange information and share resources such as files, applications, or internet connectivity.
- **Node**: Any device connected to a network that can transmit, receive, or relay data is known as a node. Examples include smartphones, laptops, servers, smart gadgets, printers, and other connected equipment.
- **Networking Devices**: These are special devices that help control, connect, and manage communication in a network. Common examples are routers, switches, hubs, and wireless access points.
- **Transmission Media**: This is the pathway through which data travels from one device to another within a network. It may be physical (wired) or non-physical (wireless).
    - **Wired Media**: Examples include Ethernet cables and fiber-optic cables used for stable and high-speed communication.
    - **Wireless Media**: Examples include Wi-Fi, Bluetooth, and infrared signals that enable communication without physical cables.
- **Service Provider Networks**: These are networks owned and managed by external organizations that provide connectivity services to individuals or companies. Examples Service provider networks include organizations such as internet service providers (ISPs), telecommunications companies, and mobile network operators that deliver network access to users.

Working of Computer Network

A computer network functions through the interaction of two main components: **nodes** and **links**.

- **Network Node**: A node is any device that participates in a network by sending, receiving, or processing data. Examples include routers, computers, modems, servers, switches, and mobile devices.
- **Link**: A link refers to the communication pathway that connects nodes. These pathways may consist of wired connections like cables or wireless technologies like radio signals or Wi-Fi.

- **Working**: Data travels across the network following a set of communication rules known as **protocols**. To ensure proper data delivery, every device in the network is assigned a distinctive identifier called an **IP address**, which acts like its digital address.
- **Firewall**: A firewall is a protective system implemented as software or hardware that oversees network traffic. It filters incoming and outgoing data and decides, based on predefined security policies, whether to permit, block, or discard the information.

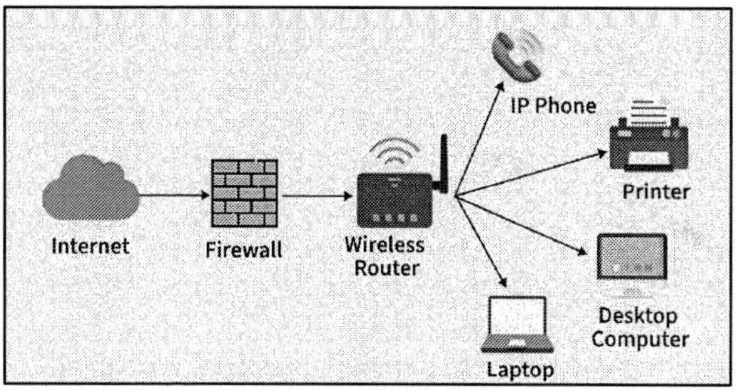

Fig 1.2 Working of Network

Types of Computer Network Architecture

Categories of Computer Network Architecture

Client–Server Architecture

Client–Server architecture is a network model in which devices are categorized as **clients** or **servers**. In this setup, the server controls access to services and resources, while client devices depend on the server for requested data, applications, or tasks. This model forms the basis of many modern technologies such as websites, cloud computing, and email services.

Operational Framework of the Client–Server Model

- **Client**:

A client refers to a device or application that starts a communication session by sending a request to the server. Clients rely on servers for services such as data retrieval, storage, or processing. Examples of client-side applications are:

- Web browsers like Chrome and Firefox
- Email software such as Gmail and Outlook

- **Server**:

A server is a dedicated machine or software system designed to respond to client requests. It delivers data, hosts applications, and performs tasks on behalf of multiple clients at the same time. Typical types of servers include:

- **Web Servers** (e.g., Apache, Nginx)
- **Email Servers**
- **Database Servers**

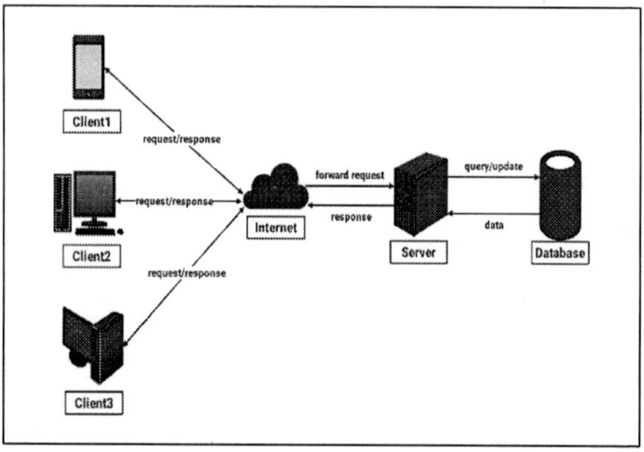

Fig. 1.3 Client Server Model

Understanding the Communication Process Between a Browser and a Server

When a user visits a website, several actions take place behind the scenes. The browser and server work together through the following steps:

1. **Entering the URL:** The user types a web address (such as www.example.com) into the browser's search or address bar. This URL tells the browser which website it should request.

2. **DNS (Domain Name System) Resolution**: The browser contacts a

DNS service to translate the human-readable domain name into a machine-readable IP address. This IP address identifies the server that hosts the requested website.

3. **Connection and Request**: After obtaining the IP address, the browser establishes communication with the server and sends a request for the webpage using HTTP or HTTPS protocols.
4. **Server Sends Data**: The server locates the requested resources and responds by sending web content such as HTML pages, CSS styles, scripts, and media files (images, videos, etc.).
5. **Browser Displays the Page**: Once the data is received, the browser interprets and displays it using different internal components:
   - **DOM Processor**: Reads and structures HTML content to build the page layout.
   - **CSS Parser**: Applies formatting and visual styles.
   - **JavaScript Engine**: Executes scripts to add dynamic features and user interaction, often using Just-In-Time (JIT) compilation to speed up execution.

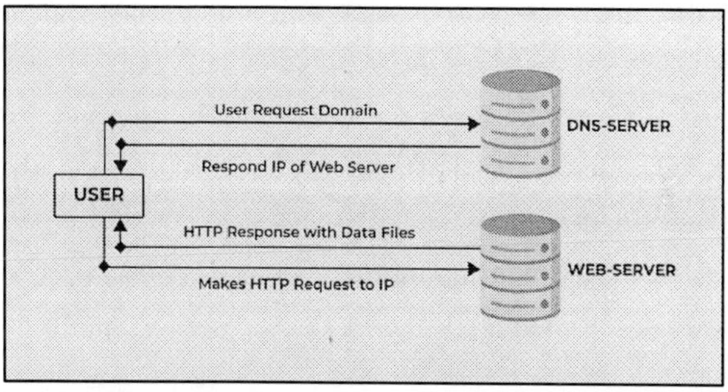

Fig 1.4 Client Server Request and Response

Real-World Examples of the Client-Server Model

Table 1.1

Use Case	Client	Server	Function
Email	Gmail, Outlook	Gmail/Yahoo Mail Servers	Send/receive email messages
Web Browsing	Chrome, Firefox	Apache, Nginx	Access and display websites
Cloud Storage	PC, Mobile App	Google Drive, Dropbox Servers	Upload/download and sync files

Advantages of the Client-Server Model

- **Centralized Data Control**: All information is stored in one main location, making updates, maintenance, and backup processes simpler and more organized.
- **Reduced Client Hardware Cost**: Client devices don't need to be highly powerful since most processing and storage tasks are handled by the server.
- **Supports Growth Easily**: New clients or additional server resources can be added without affecting the entire network, allowing both sides to expand independently.
- **Strong Security Management**: Security rules, user access, and authentication can be managed from a central server, making it easier to protect data.
- **Simplified Backup and Restoration**: Since the data resides in one central place, recovering or restoring lost information becomes faster and more efficient.

Disadvantages of Client-Server Model

- **Risk to Clients**: If a server provides malicious or infected files, client devices may become compromised, leading to malware attacks.

- **Server Becomes a Prime Target**: Attackers often focus on the server because it handles critical data and services, making it vulnerable to disruptions like DDoS (Distributed Denial of Service) assaults.
- **Possibility of Data Alteration**: When data is not properly encrypted, it can be modified while being transmitted across the network, resulting in data manipulation or tampering.
- **Man-in-the-Middle (MITM) Threats**: In the absence of secure connections, attackers can intercept communication between clients and servers, read sensitive information, or alter the exchanged data.

Peer-to-Peer (P2P) Architecture

In a **Peer-to-Peer (P2P) network**, there is no central authority or dedicated server that controls data or services. Every device connected to the network, known as a **peer**, can behave both as a **client** and a **server**. Nodes communicate directly with one another, allowing them to share files, bandwidth, storage, or any other resource without depending on a central machine. Since each participant has equal responsibility, the workload is distributed evenly across the network.

Explanation of Peer-to-Peer (P2P) Service Model

A Peer-to-Peer service refers to a simple network in which each computer can store and share files directly with other connected systems. This concept first appeared in the late 1970s. Instead of storing information on a single centralized machine, each peer stores its own data and can both provide and request resources.

Because the network does not rely on a central server, it can handle large volumes of information. Also, network reliability is higher because for the system to fail completely, **every node must stop working**, as each peer operates independently.

History of P2P Networks

- **1979 – USENET** Before P2P systems became popular, USENET provided a decentralized method for users to share articles and messages. Unlike modern forums, it did not use a single server; instead, messages were copied to various servers in the network.

- **1980s – First Practical Use** With personal computers becoming widespread, early P2P concepts started to develop among small user groups.
- **August 1988 – Internet Relay Chat (IRC)** IRC introduced one of the earliest peer-based communication systems for text messaging and real-time chat.
- **June 1999 – Napster** Napster popularized P2P file sharing, especially for music. Despite being shut down due to illegal content distribution, it made P2P technology widely recognized.
- **June 2000 – Gnutella** Gnutella introduced the first fully decentralized P2P sharing system, allowing users to share files directly without a central server.

Types of P2P Networks

1. **Unstructured P2P Networks**
   - Devices connect randomly without any specific organization.
   - Easy to build but difficult to search for specific files efficiently.
   - Examples: *Napster, Gnutella.*
2. **Structured P2P Networks**
   - Built using special algorithms that arrange nodes in a particular pattern.
   - Harder to design but provides faster and more accurate data search.
   - Examples: *P-Grid, Kademlia.*
3. **Hybrid P2P Networks**
   - A combination of client-server and P2P systems.
   - A central server may help find peers, while file sharing still occurs directly between nodes.

Features of P2P Networks

- These networks usually contain a small number of devices (commonly fewer than a dozen), and every system stores its own data; however, stored information can be accessed by other members of the group.
- Every peer can use shared resources and, at the same time, contribute its own resources, meaning overall capacity increases as more devices join.
- Since each peer can be both a provider and a requester, security risks are higher due to potential attacks on any node.
- Most modern operating systems support P2P communication and file sharing.

P2P Network Architecture

In a P2P architecture, computers connect in a workgroup to share files, printers, and internet access without a dedicated central server. Each peer has equal capabilities and responsibilities.

- Devices share information directly without requiring approval from a central authority.
- Every node acts both as a server and a client.
- Ideal for home networks, small offices, or companies where individual computers store their own data locally.
- Peers can exchange data freely across the network.
- Commonly implemented in small networks, although it may also grow beyond 12 systems depending on usage.

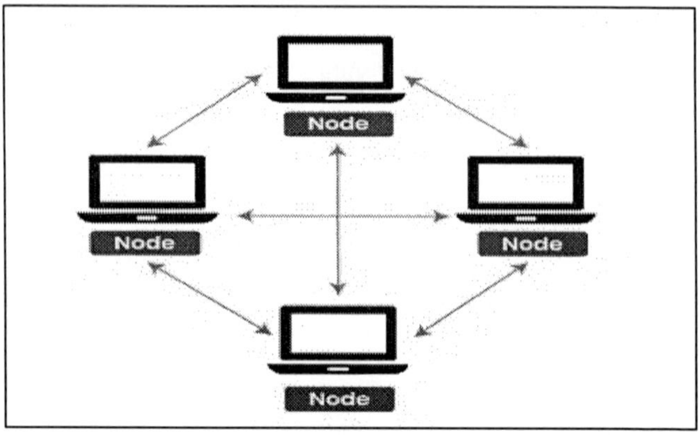

Fig. 1.5 P2P Architecture

Understanding the Functioning of a Peer-to-Peer (P2P) Network

To understand how a P2P network functions, consider a user who wants to download a file using P2P technology:

- If the user doesn't already have P2P software installed, they must first install an application that supports peer-to-peer file sharing.
- After installation, the software forms a virtual network by connecting the user's device to other P2P users.
- When the user requests a file, small pieces of that file are downloaded from multiple computers that already possess it within the network.
- At the same time, the user's system may also upload data to other peers that request files stored on their computer.

Therefore, file transfer activities in a P2P network are distributed among all connected peers, rather than being handled by a single server.

Strategies for Maintaining Security and Performance in P2P Networks

Using P2P networks safely requires precautionary measures to prevent legal and security issues. Below are best practices:

- **Download Only Legal Content**: Verify that shared or downloaded files are legitimate and don't violate copyright laws.

- **Plan a Secure Sharing Strategy**: Create policies for how files and applications should be shared to maintain data consistency and reduce risks.
- **Stay Updated with Security Tools**: Monitor emerging cyber threats and frequently update P2P software and antivirus solutions to avoid exploitation.
- **Scan Every Download**: Regularly check downloaded files for viruses and report unsafe content to IT personnel.
- **Properly Exit the Software After Use**: Completely shut down the P2P program after downloading files to prevent unauthorized access from outsiders.

Reasons Behind the Growing Popularity of P2P Services

P2P services are widely adopted because they eliminate the need for a centralized server. This architecture allows devices to interact directly, reducing operational costs and improving reliability. During file sharing, data fragments are fetched from multiple peers, improving speed and efficiency. The decentralized structure also makes the system harder to shut down completely.

Applications of P2P Networks

Some common uses of P2P architecture include:

- **File Sharing**: A cost-effective method of distributing files without relying on a central server.
- **Blockchain Technology**: Blockchain networks use P2P principles so that every node maintains identical records, enhancing transparency and security.
- **Secure Messaging**: Encrypted peer-to-peer messaging systems offer fast and protected communication between users.
- **Collaboration**: Easy sharing of digital resources promotes teamwork within small or large networks.
- **Popular File-Sharing Platforms**: Networks like G2 and eDonkey

popularized P2P file transfer.

- **Content Distribution**: Unlike client–server networks, P2P users can both request and supply data, increasing distribution capacity as users grow.
- **IP Telephony**: Applications such as Skype use P2P concepts to handle voice communication over the internet.

Examples of P2P Networks

P2P systems can operate at three levels:

1. **Basic Level** – Simple two-device connections using USB or direct link cables.
2. **Intermediate Level** – Multiple systems connected via cables like copper wiring.
3. **Advanced Level** – Software-driven P2P applications managing many devices across the internet.

Popular P2P platforms include **BitTorrent, Gnutella, eDonkey, Kasaa, Napster, and Skype**.

Advantages of P2P Networks

- **Simple Maintenance**: Each device manages itself; no central administration is required.
- **Cost Reduction**: No need to purchase an expensive server since every computer contributes resources.
- **No Dedicated Network Administrator**: Every user controls their own system.
- **Flexible Expansion**: Adding, removing, or fixing devices is straightforward.
- **Lower Traffic Load**: Resource sharing is distributed, reducing overall congestion.

Disadvantages of P2P Networks

- **Risk of Data Loss**: Due to the lack of centralized backup, data may be lost if devices fail.

- **Weaker Security**: Maintaining full security is challenging since every user controls their own node.
- **Performance Issues**: A device can slow down when other peers frequently request files from it.
- **Difficult to Locate Resources**: Without a central directory, files stored on individual systems may be harder to find.

Fundamentals of Network Devices

A computer network connects multiple hosts to exchange information through various communication paths. To enable communication between these devices, specialized hardware known as **network devices** is used. These include:

- **Routers**
- **Switches**
- **Hubs**
- **Bridges**

These devices help transmit data efficiently between two or more systems within a network.

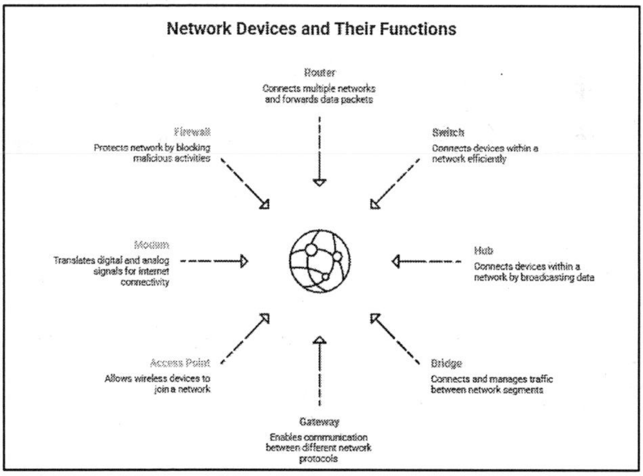

Fig. 1.6 Network Devices

Network Devices and Their Functions

1. **Router**
   - A router links multiple networks, such as a home network and the internet.
   - It forwards data packets to their intended destinations using intelligent routing techniques.
2. **Switch**
   - A switch connects multiple devices within the same network, such as computers in a company.
   - Unlike a hub, it sends data only to the specific device for which it is meant, improving speed and efficiency.
3. **Hub**
   - A hub is a basic networking device used to connect several systems within a network.
   - It broadcasts data to all connected devices, making it less efficient compared to a switch.
4. **Bridge**
   - A bridge is used to connect and manage traffic between two different network segments.
   - It helps minimize congestion by filtering unnecessary data.
5. **Gateway**
   - A gateway enables communication between networks that use different communication protocols.
   - It converts data formats, acting as a translator between two dissimilar systems.
6. **Access Point (AP)**
   - An access point allows wireless devices to join a network.
   - It extends a wired network to create a Wi-Fi zone.
7. **Modem**
   - A modem translates digital signals from a computer into analog signals suitable for telephone or cable lines and vice versa.
   - It plays a key role in providing internet connectivity.

8. **Firewall**
   - A firewall supervises incoming and outgoing network traffic.
   - It protects a network by blocking malicious activities and unauthorized access.

Computer Network – Meaning

A computer network is a setup that links multiple independent devices, such as computers, printers, and servers, to exchange information and share resources effortlessly. Networks can be formed using wired connections (cables) or wireless technologies. Both hardware components and software tools are essential to build and manage a network system. By communicating through a network, users can access shared services, collaborate, and retrieve information efficiently.

Goals of Computer Networks

- **Convenience:** To make computing easier and more user-friendly.
- **Efficiency:** To allow hardware and software resources to be used optimally.
- **Resource Management:** To properly distribute CPU time, memory, storage, and I/O devices among users.
- **Security & Protection:** To safeguard resources and data against unauthorized access or damage.
- **Reliability & Fault Tolerance:** To ensure continuous network operation even when failures occur.
- **Scalability:** To support the growing number of users, devices, and services without compromising performance.

Uses of Computer Networks

- **Communication:** Enables services like email, instant messaging, and video conferencing.
- **Resource Sharing:** Allows multiple users to share devices such as scanners, printers, and storage systems.

- **Remote Access:** Permits users to access systems and information from distant locations.
- **Collaboration:** Makes it easy to work together on documents and projects in real time.
- **E-commerce:** Supports secure online transactions and digital marketplaces.
- **Education:** Facilitates online learning platforms, research activities, and interactive teaching.

Characteristics of Computer Networks

1. **Security**
   - Networks implement techniques such as authentication, encryption, and firewall protection to secure data from threats and unauthorized use.
2. **Reliability**
   - A reliable network ensures continuous availability of data and services. Backup systems and redundant paths help maintain operations during failures.
3. **Scalability**
   - Networks should adapt to growth in users and devices without affecting performance. For instance, the internet handles millions of new connections every day.
4. **High Performance**
   - Efficient bandwidth, minimal delay, and high throughput contribute to better network performance. These factors determine how quickly data is processed and transferred.
5. **Quality of Service (QoS)**
   - QoS prioritizes critical data, ensuring smooth performance for applications such as online meetings, streaming, and real-time communication.

1.2 Networks Types

Computer networks can be categorized based on size, communication method, geographical coverage, ownership, transmission technology, and architecture. One common classification is based on the coverage area:

1. Personal Area Network (PAN)

A Personal Area Network is the smallest type of network used for communication among personal electronic devices located close to an individual. It typically covers a range of about 1 to 10 meters. PAN connects smartphones, smartwatches, laptops, tablets, and other portable devices for easy sharing and communication. The network is inexpensive, easy to manage, and offers fast communication.

Examples of PAN:

- A Bluetooth connection between a smartphone and wireless earbuds.
- Infrared communication between a remote control and a television.

Fig. 1.7 Personal Area Network

2. Local Area Network (LAN)

A Local Area Network, commonly known as LAN, is one of the most widely used types of networks. It connects multiple computers and other devices within a restricted space, such as a home, school, laboratory, or office building. Devices in a LAN communicate using a shared communication channel and often operate through a central server. Technologies such as **Ethernet** and **Wi-Fi** are mainly used to establish LAN connections. LANs typically cover an area of up to **2 kilometers**, offering **high-speed data transfer**, **simple management**, and **cost-effective installation**.

Examples of LAN:

- Wireless LAN used in homes, schools, or cafés.
- Wired network connections in corporate offices.

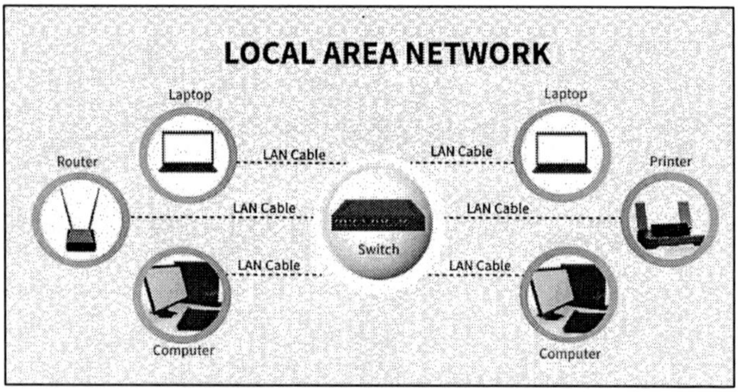

Fig. 1.8 Local Area Network

3. Campus Area Network (CAN)

A Campus Area Network, or CAN, is a network larger than a Local Area Network (LAN) but smaller than a Metropolitan Area Network (MAN). This type of network is typically deployed within educational or organizational campuses, such as universities, schools, or corporate office complexes. CAN connects multiple buildings within the same campus and enables high-speed communication between them. It generally operates using **Ethernet technology**, supports a **range of several kilometers**, and offers **fast data transfer** with **moderate setup and maintenance costs**.

Examples of CAN:

- Networks linking different departments or buildings in schools or colleges.
- Connectivity across multiple structures in a corporate or research campus.

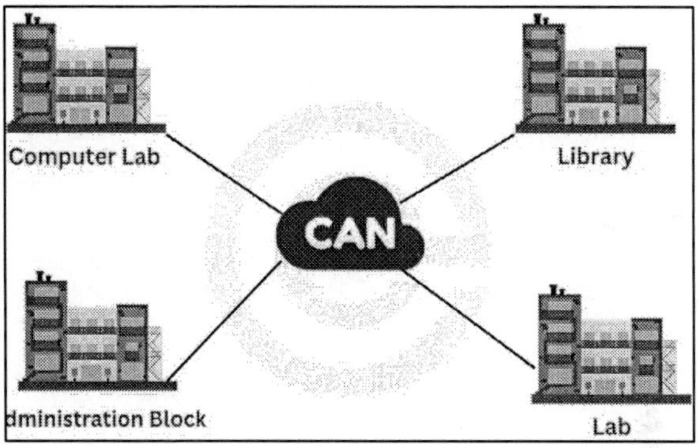

Fig. 1.9 Campus Area Network

4. Metropolitan Area Network (MAN)

A Metropolitan Area Network, commonly known as MAN, is a network that spans a larger area than a Local Area Network (LAN) but is smaller in scale compared to a Wide Area Network (WAN). It is designed to connect computers and network resources across a city, large town, or metropolitan zone using a shared communication medium. MANs generally rely on technologies such as **FDDI (Fiber Distributed Data Interface), CDDI (Copper Distributed Data Interface), and ATM (Asynchronous Transfer Mode)**. These networks typically cover distances ranging from **5 km to 50 km**. Although they provide **moderate transmission speeds**, they require **complex management and incur higher installation and maintenance costs**.

Examples of MAN:

- Network systems deployed across an entire city
- Communication links connecting multiple public buildings or offices within a large urban region

- City-level internet service provider networks

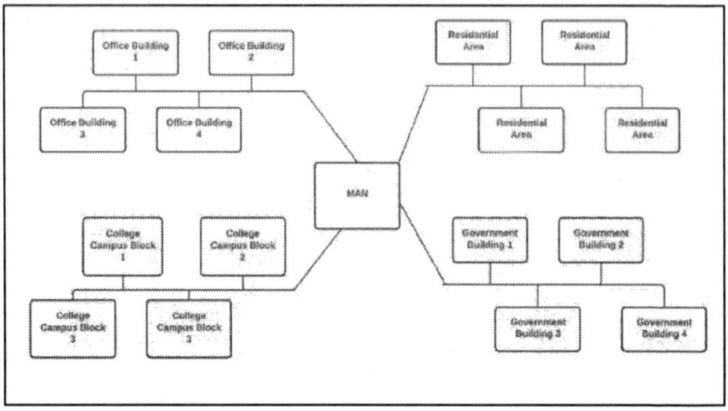

Fig. 1.10 Metropolitan Area Network (MAN)

5. Wide Area Network (WAN)

A Wide Area Network, or WAN, is a computer network that connects systems across a **large geographical area**, often spanning cities, countries, or even continents. Unlike LAN or MAN, WAN is not restricted to a single location and can link multiple local area networks together. WANs commonly use technologies such as **leased lines** and **dial-up connections**. These networks typically cover distances **beyond 50 km**, offer **lower transmission speeds**, and involve **high installation and maintenance costs**.

Examples of WAN:

- The **Internet**, which is the largest WAN in the world.
- Banking networks connecting branches across different countries.
- Global corporate networks linking offices in multiple cities.

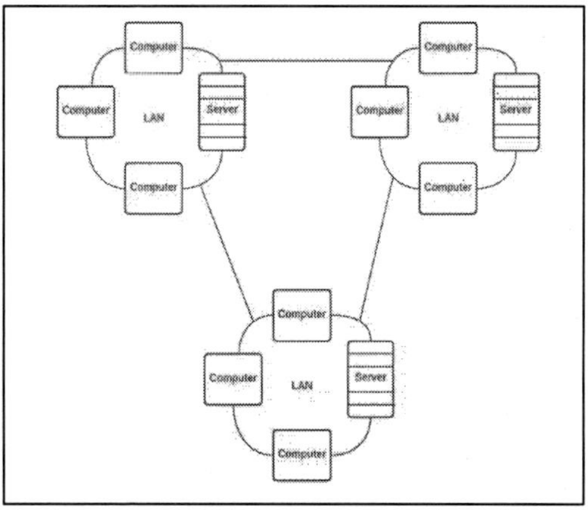

Fig. 1.11 Wide Area Network (WAN)

1.3 Layered Network Models

- Layered architecture in computer networks refers to dividing a network's functioning into different layers, each responsible for a certain communication component. The major goal of this layered architecture is to separate the complex network communication process into manageable, smaller activities that can be better developed. In this article, we will discuss Layered Architecture in Introduction to Layered Architecture

In computer networks, a layered architecture is a design approach where the overall network process is divided into **smaller, manageable sub-tasks**, each assigned to a specific **layer**. Each layer is responsible for performing only its **dedicated functions**. Lower layers provide services to the layers above them, allowing higher layers to build on these functions to deliver complete network services to clients.

This structured approach enables **interaction between different sub-systems** while keeping each layer independent. Consequently, any changes or modifications made in one layer do not affect the operations of other layers, making the network more **flexible, modular, and easier to manage**.

A **layered architecture** divides the complex process of networking into smaller, manageable **sub-tasks**, each assigned to a dedicated layer. Each layer focuses on a specific task and provides services to the layer above it. Data moves from one layer to the next, while the **physical medium** at the bottom ensures actual transmission occurs. This structure simplifies communication and allows changes in one layer without affecting others.

Features of Layered Architecture

- **Modularity and Clear Interfaces:** Each layer has defined responsibilities, making it easier to understand and manage.
- **Layer Independence:** Layers provide services to higher layers without revealing how these services are implemented.
- **Segmentation of Complex Tasks:** Large, complicated processes are broken into smaller sub-tasks, each handled by a separate layer.
- **Physical Communication:** The physical layer (layer 1) provides the actual path for data transfer.
- **Flexible Implementation:** Modifications in one layer do not affect others, allowing easier updates and maintenance.

Elements of Layered Architecture

1. **Service:** Functions provided by a lower layer to support higher layers. Each layer has distinct services tailored to its responsibilities.
2. **Protocol:** A set of rules that govern how layers communicate and transmit data to their peer layers. It defines the format, sequence, and error handling of data.
3. **Interface:** The channel or mechanism through which data and messages pass between adjacent layers.

Significance of Layered Architecture

- **Divide and Conquer:** Complex network operations are split into smaller sub-tasks, reducing overall complexity.
- **Ease of Modification:** Changes in one layer do not impact other layers, allowing smooth updates.
- **Modularity:** Each layer is independent, making the architecture

easy to understand, implement, and maintain.

- **Testing:** Layers can be tested individually, simplifying problem detection and debugging.
- **Scalability:** New layers or protocols can be added as networks grow, without disrupting existing operations.
- **Security:** Layered design allows implementing security measures at multiple levels.
- **Efficiency:** Each layer focuses on specific tasks, optimizing resource utilization and performance.

Evolution of Layered Architecture

Layered architectures are fundamental to modern network communication. Two major models using this approach are:

- **OSI Model**
- **TCP/IP Model**

OSI Model (Open Systems Interconnection)

The OSI Model is a **seven-layered architecture** where each layer performs a distinct role in data transmission:

1. **Physical Layer:** The lowest layer responsible for the physical connection between devices. Data is transmitted as bits. Functions include bit rate control, synchronization, and transmission mode.
2. **Data Link Layer:** Ensures error-free delivery of messages from one node to another. Performs framing, flow control, and error detection/correction.
3. **Network Layer:** Handles transmission of data between hosts in different networks. Functions include routing and logical addressing.
4. **Transport Layer:** Provides reliable delivery of data from the network layer to the application layer. Tasks include segmentation, reassembly, and service point addressing.
5. **Session Layer:** Manages communication sessions between devices. Functions include session establishment, maintenance, synchronization, and termination.

6. **Presentation Layer:** Acts as a translation layer, converting data from the application layer into a suitable format. Performs encryption, decryption, compression, and data translation.

7. **Application Layer:** The topmost layer, also called the user layer, provides network services directly to applications. Examples include directory services, email, and network virtual terminals.

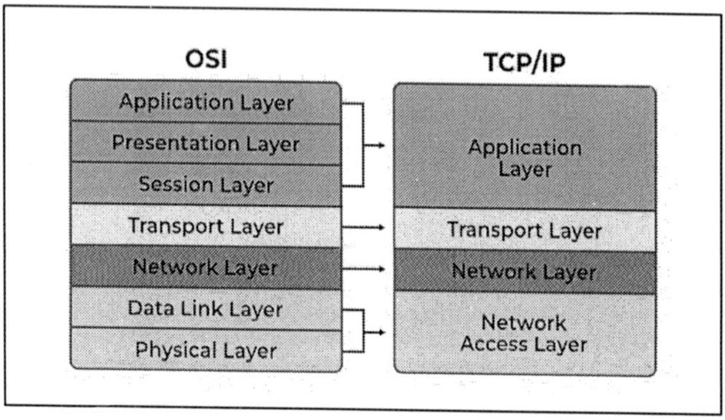

Fig. 1.12 OSI and TCP/IP

TCP/IP Model

The **TCP/IP model** is a framework for computer networks that defines how data is transmitted between devices. Unlike the OSI model, it has four layers, each responsible for specific tasks in communication.

1. Network Access Layer

- This layer handles the physical transmission of data over the network.
- It is responsible for creating and delivering data packets, framing, and error detection.
- It also identifies the network protocol type (TCP/IP) for the packets.
- Examples of data link layer protocols used here include **Point-to-Point Protocol (PPP)** and **Ethernet IEEE 802.2**.

2. Internet Layer

- The Internet layer is similar to the OSI network layer.
- It ensures **logical transmission of data** across different networks.
- Key protocols include:
  - **IP (Internet Protocol):** Delivers packets from the source to the destination using IP addresses. IPv4 is currently the most common, but IPv6 is gradually replacing it due to address limitations.
  - **ICMP (Internet Control Message Protocol):** Provides error messages and information about network issues.
  - **ARP (Address Resolution Protocol):** Maps a known IP address to a hardware (MAC) address. Variants include Reverse ARP, Proxy ARP, Gratuitous ARP, and Inverse ARP.

3. Transport Layer

- Ensures **reliable data transfer** and maintains the order of packets.
- Provides **end-to-end communication** between applications.
- Main protocols:
  - **TCP (Transmission Control Protocol):** Provides reliable, connection-oriented communication, sending data in order and ensuring all packets arrive.
  - **UDP (User Datagram Protocol):** Provides connectionless communication for small amounts of data. It is faster than TCP but does not guarantee delivery or order.

4. Application Layer

- The top layer responsible for **end-to-end communication** and providing network services to applications.
- Protects applications from the complexities of lower layers.
- Key protocols include:
  - **HTTP/HTTPS:** Manage communication between web browsers and servers. HTTPS adds encryption via SSL for secure transactions.
  - **SSH (Secure Shell):** Provides encrypted terminal access, preferred

over Telnet for security.

- **NTP (Network Time Protocol):** Synchronizes device clocks to a standard time source, ensuring consistency in transactions and logging.

Benefits of Layered Architecture

- **Modularity:** Tasks are divided into manageable layers.
- **Interoperability:** Different systems can work together.
- **Flexibility:** Layers can be modified independently.
- **Reusability:** Protocols and services can be reused across layers.
- **Scalability:** Supports network growth without redesigning the system.
- **Security:** Easier to implement security measures at multiple layers.

Challenges of Layered Architecture

- **Performance Overhead:** Extra processing due to multiple layers.
- **Implementation Complexity:** Requires careful coordination between layers.
- **Resource Utilization:** More layers may consume more memory and CPU.
- **Debugging and Troubleshooting:** Errors can occur at any layer, complicating diagnosis.
- **Protocol Overhead:** Additional data added for communication between layers.

Real-World Applications

- Internet browsing and web services
- Email communication
- Video streaming platforms
- Online gaming networks
- Voice over IP (VoIP) services
- Smart home devices and automation
- Cloud computing infrastructure
- Blockchain networks

1.4 Emergence of Internet of Things (IoT)- Introduction

The **Internet of Things (IoT)** is a network of **interconnected physical objects**, such as devices, machines, vehicles, or even people. These objects are equipped with **sensors, software, and unique identifiers** that enable them to **collect, exchange, and process data** over a network without requiring direct human-to-human or human-to-computer interaction.

IoT enables **automation, real-time monitoring, and smart decision-making** in areas like healthcare, transportation, smart homes, industrial automation, and environmental monitoring.

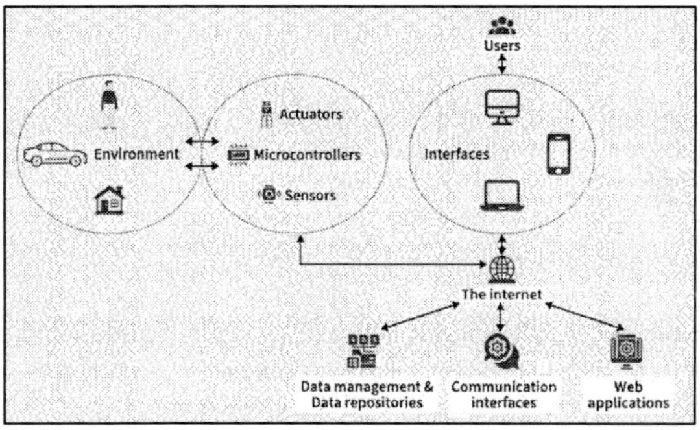

Fig. 1.13 IOT Ecosystem

IoT involves **connecting physical devices** to the internet to collect, share, and analyze data. Sensors in these devices gather information from the environment and transmit it to **edge devices or cloud platforms**, where it is processed and analyzed. The results are then either presented to users through apps or used to automatically control actuators and systems.

Components of an IoT System

IoT systems rely on four key components working together to enable smart decision-making and automation:

1. **Devices & Sensors**

- Physical objects equipped with sensors or actuators that monitor environmental parameters such as temperature, motion, gas, or light.

- Sensors convert physical signals into digital data that can be analyzed.

2. **Connectivity**

- Networks like **Wi-Fi, Bluetooth, Zigbee, LoRaWAN, and 5G** transmit data between devices, gateways, and cloud platforms.

3. **Data Processing**

- Data collected by sensors is processed on **edge devices, gateways, or cloud platforms**, often using **AI or big data analytics**.
- This step transforms raw data into actionable insights.

4. **User Interface (UI)**

- Applications, dashboards, or mobile apps allow users to monitor, control, and interact with IoT systems.
- User interfaces can also trigger actuators to perform automated actions.

Note: Modern IoT devices often rely on **low-power embedded systems**, which provide high performance while minimizing energy consumption

Types of Sensors in IoT

- **Temperature Sensors:** Measure heat or temperature changes.
- **Image Sensors:** Capture visual data for cameras or computer vision.
- **Gyroscope (Gyro) Sensors:** Detect angular velocity and object orientation.
- **Obstacle Sensors:** Identify obstacles to prevent collisions.
- **RF Sensors:** Use radio frequency for detection, tracking, or communication.
- **Infrared (IR) Sensors:** Detect heat signatures or motion.
- **MQ Gas Sensors (MQ-2/5):** Detect gases such as CO, methane, or smoke.
- **LDR (Light Dependent Resistor) Sensors:** Measure light intensity.

- **Ultrasonic Sensors:** Calculate distances using ultrasonic waves.

IoT Enablers

These are key technologies that make IoT possible:

- **RFID & NFC:** Enable automatic object identification and tracking via radio waves or short-range communication.
- **Sensor Technologies:** Convert environmental parameters into digital data.
- **Low-Power Embedded Systems:** Minimize energy consumption while maintaining reliability.
- **Smart Networks & Protocols:** Protocols like **MQTT, CoAP, Zigbee, and 5G** ensure fast, reliable data transfer.
- **Cloud & Big Data:** Platforms for storing, managing, and analyzing large volumes of IoT data.
- **Edge/Fog Computing:** Localized processing near devices to reduce latency, save bandwidth, and improve response times.

Working Mechanism of IoT Devices

1. **Data Collection & Transmission:** Sensors gather environmental or operational data and transmit it via the network.
2. **Actuation:** Actuators perform actions based on triggers from sensors or processed data, automating tasks according to user-defined conditions.
3. **Information Reception:** Devices or users can receive relevant data from the network for analysis or control purposes.
4. **Communication Assistance:** IoT devices communicate with each other or across networks using protocols such as **MQTT, CoAP, Zigbee, FTP, HTTP**, enabling seamless interaction and data exchange.

IoT enables **smart automation, real-time monitoring, and data-driven decision-making**, making it critical for applications in **smart homes, healthcare, industrial automation, transportation, and environmental monitoring**.

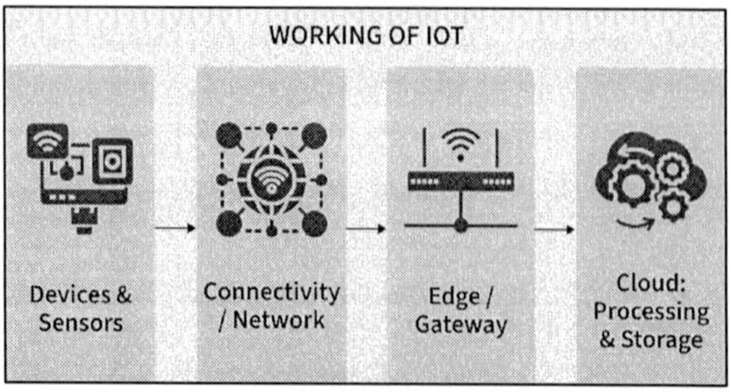

Fig. 1.14 Working of IOT

Characteristics of IoT

- **Always Connected:** IoT devices maintain constant connectivity but often enter low-power or sleep modes to conserve energy, waking only when required.
- **Interoperable:** They can communicate with a variety of other devices, regardless of hardware or software differences, ensuring smooth interaction.
- **Adaptive:** IoT devices can adjust to changing conditions—for example, a smart light increasing brightness as the room gets darker.
- **Intelligent:** Beyond data collection, these devices analyze information to provide actionable insights, like a fitness tracker offering health recommendations based on activity data.
- **Scalable:** IoT systems can expand from a few devices to thousands without losing performance or efficiency.
- **Energy-Efficient:** Devices manage power consumption effectively, activating only when necessary to save battery life.

Modern Applications of IoT

- **Smart Grids:** Optimizing energy distribution and consumption.
- **Smart Cities:** Enhancing urban infrastructure, traffic management, and public services.
- **Smart Homes:** Automating lighting, security, climate control, and

appliances.

- **Healthcare:** Remote monitoring, wearable health trackers, and telemedicine.
- **Disaster Detection:** Earthquake monitoring and early warning systems.
- **Hazard Monitoring:** Detection of radiation or harmful gases.
- **Mobile Device Tracking:** Locating and managing smartphones and connected devices.

Advantages of IoT

- Streamlines processes, improving efficiency and automation.
- Provides greater convenience and easy access to information.
- Enables real-time monitoring and control of devices and systems.

Disadvantages of IoT

- **Security Risks:** Vulnerable to hacking and cyberattacks.
- **Privacy Issues:** Potential misuse of personal or sensitive data.
- **High Costs:** Initial setup and maintenance can be expensive.

1.5 Evolution of IOT (Internet of Things)

The phrase **"Internet of Things"** was first coined by computer scientist **Kevin Ashton in 1999**. While working at Procter & Gamble, Ashton proposed using special chips to track products throughout the supply chain. He chose the term "internet" to attract attention, as it was a widely recognized buzzword at the time.

IoT quickly gained traction among major companies:

- **LG** released its first smart refrigerator in 2000.
- **Apple** launched the first iPhone seven years later.

By **2008**, the number of connected devices worldwide had already surpassed the global population, highlighting the rapid growth of IoT.

Wireless Sensor Networks and RFID (2000–2010)

The introduction of **Radio Frequency Identification (RFID)** and **Wireless Sensor Networks (WSN)** was pivotal in IoT development.

These technologies enabled devices to communicate, collect data, and function reliably, laying the foundation for modern IoT systems used today.

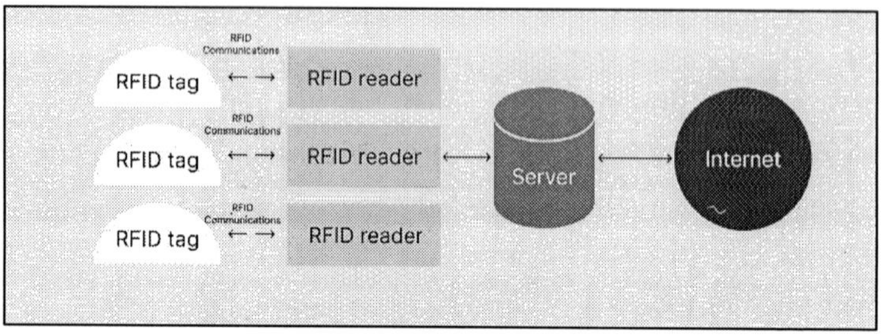

Fig. 1.15 RFID Technology

For instance, **RFID tags** are frequently attached to items to enable real-time tracking of their location using high-frequency radio signals. This technology is widely applied in **asset management systems** to monitor inventory and equipment efficiently.

The term **Wireless Sensor Network (WSN)** refers to a collection of distributed sensors designed to observe and record environmental conditions or other specific parameters. These sensors transmit the collected data to dedicated platforms or servers for processing. WSNs serve as a critical component for many **IoT applications**, forming the backbone of their monitoring and data-collection capabilities.

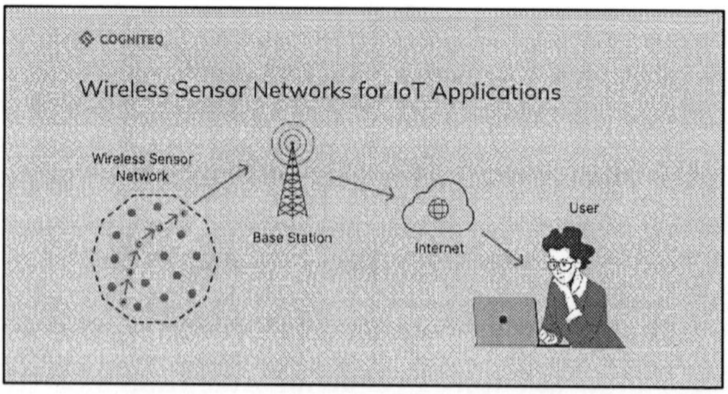

Fig. 1.16 Wireless Sensor Network

Smart Homes and Consumer IoT (2010-2015)

Smart home devices and consumer-focused IoT products, such as **smartwatches** and **voice-controlled appliances**, are now commonplace. However, not long ago, these innovations were considered groundbreaking. Over time, these technologies have become more advanced, feature-rich, and intelligent. Even the earliest versions offered clear advantages.

These solutions allow users to **automate everyday tasks**, improve **home security**, and optimize the use of resources like electricity. For example, **smart heating systems** can automatically regulate temperature based on real-time data, turning heating on or off as needed. This not only conserves energy but also maintains comfort without manual intervention. Similarly, smart lighting, smart locks, automated curtains, and other modules can be integrated into a smart home ecosystem.

To enhance safety, homes can be equipped with **sensors** that detect water leaks, fires, or unauthorized entries and alert users immediately.

Industrial IoT (IIoT) and Smart Cities (2015–2020)

In the early stages of IoT adoption, significant progress was made in **industrial applications** and **smart city initiatives**.

Industrial IoT (IIoT) solutions help optimize operational efficiency, enhance workplace safety, and improve product quality. By collecting real-time data through sensors and smart devices, managers gain better insights into equipment performance and operational conditions.

One of the most impactful IIoT applications is **predictive maintenance**. AI-enabled IoT systems can monitor equipment, analyze operational data, and identify potential failures before they occur. Notifications are sent to operators when anomalies are detected, preventing costly downtime and unexpected breakdowns.

Other industrial use cases include:

- **Asset tracking**
- **Supply chain management**

- **Inventory monitoring**
- **Remote production oversight**
- **Digital twins** – virtual replicas of physical objects or processes that simulate real-world behavior using real-time sensor data, enabling experimentation without financial risk.

Smart city technologies integrate multiple modules, such as real-time traffic management, water monitoring, and smart parking. These systems enhance urban safety with smart lighting, surveillance, and efficient resource management. While widespread adoption is limited due to high infrastructure costs, long-term benefits include lower resource consumption and improved quality of life.

5G and Edge Computing (2020–Present)

The **speed and efficiency of data transmission** are critical for IoT performance. The rollout of **5G networks** has significantly improved the quality of data processing and communication for IoT devices. Faster, low-latency connections enable real-time decision-making, smoother device interactions, and more reliable performance.

Edge computing complements this by processing data closer to where it is generated, reducing delays and network congestion. Together, 5G and edge computing allow IoT systems to operate more efficiently, supporting advanced applications in **smart homes, industries, and cities**.

Benefits of 5G for IoT

The introduction of **5G technology** has brought several advantages for IoT systems:

- **Faster data transfer**: 5G provides much higher speeds than 4G, allowing devices to communicate more efficiently.
- **Low latency**: The reduced delay in data transmission enables real-time applications and quicker responses.
- **Energy efficiency**: Connected devices, especially indoor IoT systems, benefit from improved energy-saving capabilities.
- **Better indoor coverage**: Enhanced signal penetration ensures

reliable performance in areas like basements, parking lots, and other indoor spaces.

- **Improved mobile broadband**: High-speed, reliable internet access allows for seamless operation of IoT-enabled mobile devices.

Edge Computing in IoT

Edge computing is a growing trend in IoT development. Instead of sending all data to the cloud for processing, edge computing handles data locally, close to the source. This approach reduces the time required for data processing, decreases network traffic, and increases data security. By processing information at the edge, IoT systems become faster, more reliable, and more efficient.

IoT in Healthcare and Wearables (2020–Present)

Although medical IoT solutions are relatively recent, their impact on healthcare is significant. One key application is **remote patient monitoring**, which allows continuous tracking of patient vitals without overloading healthcare staff. These systems enable timely interventions based on real-time data.

Wearable devices designed for fitness and sports can monitor health metrics during exercise or competitions. By analyzing this data, athletes and enthusiasts can improve performance and assess their health more accurately.

Advanced **medical IoT devices** such as ECG monitors and smart spirometers, often enhanced with AI and machine learning, improve diagnostic precision and patient care.

Hospital asset management is another important use case. By attaching **RFID tags** to equipment and supplies, hospitals can track the location of items in real-time. This reduces the time spent locating equipment, prevents losses, and lowers operational costs.

Future Trends and Innovations in IoT

Although IoT technology has advanced considerably, its development is ongoing. Future trends focus on **integrating IoT with emerging technologies** such as artificial intelligence, machine learning, 5G networks, edge computing, and blockchain. These integrations will make IoT systems smarter, more secure, and more capable of supporting complex applications across healthcare, industry, smart cities, and everyday life.

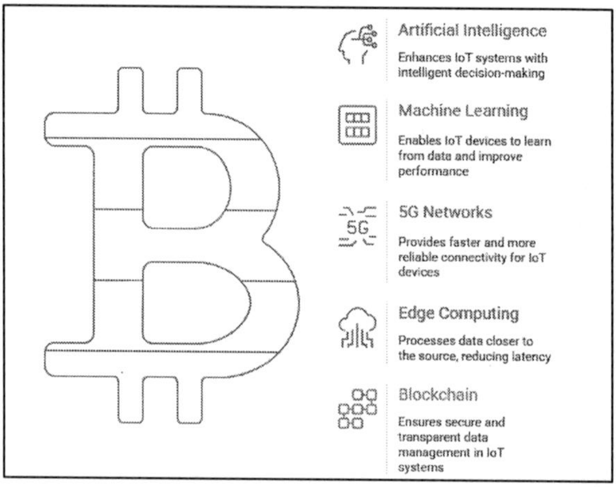

Fig. 1.17 Future Trends in IOT

Integration of IoT with Emerging Technologies

1. IoT and Artificial Intelligence (AI) Artificial Intelligence and Machine Learning are increasingly integrated into IoT systems. While IoT devices gather vast amounts of data, AI and ML algorithms analyze it to identify trends, detect anomalies, and make predictions. This combination is valuable not only for business planning but also for practical applications such as smart homes, predictive maintenance, and autonomous vehicles.

2. IoT and Augmented/Virtual Reality (AR/VR) Although AR and VR are commonly associated with gaming and entertainment, their integration with IoT opens up broader possibilities. IoT collects real-time data, which can then be visualized using AR/VR devices such as smart glasses or head-mounted displays. This combination is particularly useful in manufacturing, warehouse management, and healthcare, where high-precision operations like complex surgeries can benefit from real-time data visualization.

3. IoT and Blockchain Blockchain technology can enhance IoT systems by providing secure and tamper-resistant data storage. The use of immutable ledgers ensures data integrity and authenticity, making blockchain ideal for applications where secure, verifiable information transfer is critical

1.6 Enabling IOT Technologies

Several technologies work together to support the development and operation of IoT applications:

- **Wireless Sensor Networks (WSN)**
- **Cloud Computing**
- **Big Data Analytics**
- **Communication Protocols**
- **Embedded Systems**

Wireless Sensor Networks (WSN)

A **Wireless Sensor Network** is a collection of interconnected devices that communicate via wireless channels. WSNs consist of distributed sensors that monitor environmental or physical conditions, such as temperature, humidity, motion, or pressure.

Components of WSN:

- **End Nodes:** Devices that collect data from the environment. These nodes can also function as routers, forwarding data to other nodes.
- **Routers:** Devices that help transmit data between nodes and the coordinator.
- **Coordinator:** The central device that gathers data from all nodes and connects to the internet or other processing systems.

WSNs are fundamental to IoT, as they enable real-time monitoring, data collection, and communication across various applications.

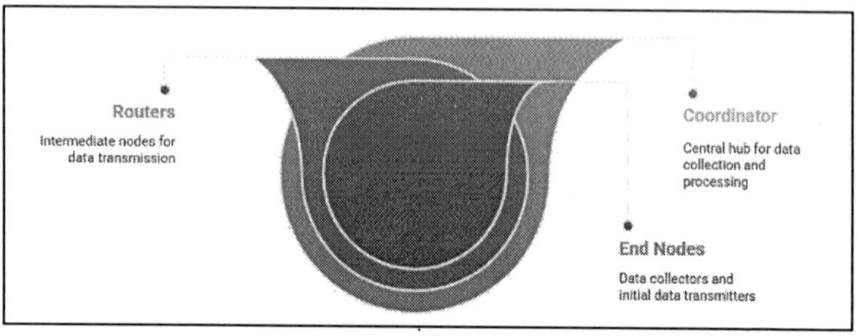

Fig. 1.18 Components of WSN

Examples of Wireless Sensor Networks (WSNs) in IoT

Wireless Sensor Networks are widely used in IoT applications across various domains. Some practical examples include:

- **Weather Monitoring Systems:** Collect real-time meteorological data such as temperature, humidity, and rainfall.
- **Indoor Air Quality Monitoring:** Track pollutants and air conditions inside buildings for health and safety.
- **Soil Moisture Monitoring:** Help in agriculture by monitoring soil conditions and optimizing irrigation.
- **Surveillance Systems:** Enable security monitoring using sensors and cameras.
- **Smart Grids:** Monitor energy distribution and usage to optimize efficiency.
- **Structural Health Monitoring:** Track the stability and integrity of buildings, bridges, and other infrastructure.

IoT Enabling Technologies: Cloud Computing

Cloud computing is a technology where computing resources, applications, and services are delivered over the Internet. Users can access compute, storage, and networking resources on demand without needing physical infrastructure. This is particularly useful in IoT for storing, processing, and analyzing massive amounts of sensor data.

Key Characteristics of Cloud Computing:

- **On-Demand Availability:** Resources automatically adjust based on workload; they scale up when demand increases and scale down when it decreases.
- **Autonomic Operation:** Cloud services require minimal human intervention as resources are dynamically allocated and managed.
- **Scalability (Elasticity):** Resources can expand or shrink based on usage, ensuring optimal performance and cost efficiency.
- **Pay-Per-Use:** Users are billed only for the resources and duration they actually use, unlike traditional fixed-cost setups.
- **Ubiquitous Access:** Cloud resources can be accessed globally from any internet-connected device, allowing seamless remote work and data retrieval.

Cloud Service Models

Cloud computing provides three main service models:

1. **Infrastructure as a Service (IaaS):** Provides foundational resources such as servers, storage, and networking for organizations to build and manage their own applications.
2. **Platform as a Service (PaaS):** Offers development tools, runtime environments, and frameworks to design, deploy, and manage applications without worrying about underlying infrastructure.
3. **Software as a Service (SaaS):** Delivers fully developed applications accessible over the Internet. Users can directly use software without installation or maintenance. Examples include **Gmail, Facebook, Dropbox, and YouTube**.

These models support the wide adoption of IoT by providing flexible, scalable, and cost-efficient infrastructure and applications.

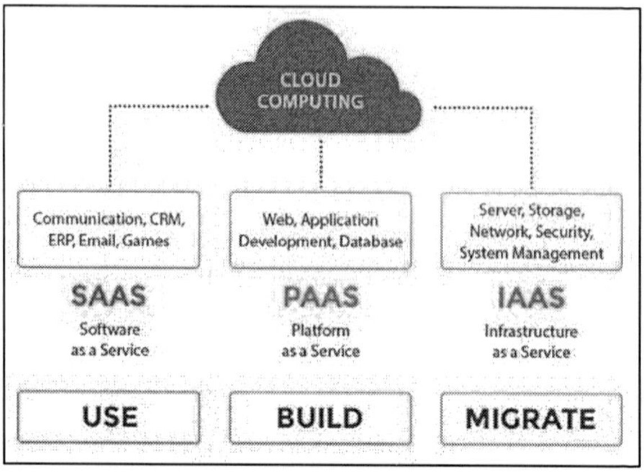

Fig. 1.19 Types of cloud service model

Cloud Deployment Models

Cloud computing can be implemented in different ways depending on who owns the infrastructure and how the services are accessed. These variations in ownership and usage form what are known as **cloud deployment models**. There are four primary deployment models used in cloud environments:

- **Public Cloud:** The cloud infrastructure is available to the general public and is owned by a third-party service provider. Anyone can subscribe to and use its services on a pay-as-you-use basis.
- **Private Cloud:** This cloud is exclusively used by a single organization. The infrastructure may be managed internally or by an external provider, but access is restricted to authorized users within that organization.
- **Community Cloud:** A cloud environment shared by multiple organizations that have similar requirements, such as security needs or industry compliance. It supports a specific group or community of users with common goals.
- **Hybrid Cloud:** A combination of two or more cloud models (public, private, or community) integrated together. It allows data and

applications to be shared between them, providing flexibility and optimized resource utilization.

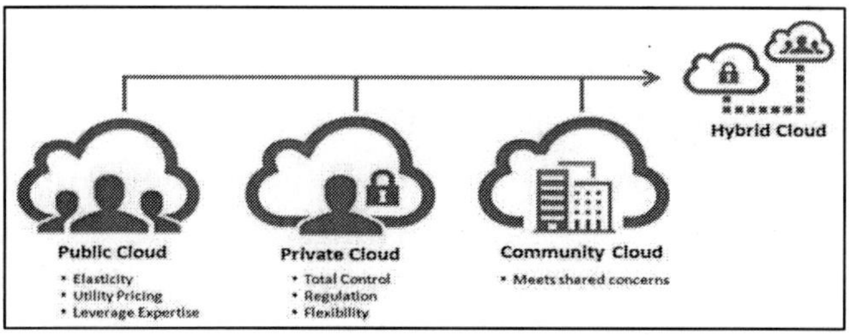

Fig. 1.20 Deployment Models

Public Cloud vs. Private Cloud

In a **public cloud environment**, computing resources such as storage, applications, and processing power are made available to multiple users on a shared basis. These services are typically hosted and operated by external cloud providers, who take complete responsibility for managing and maintaining the underlying infrastructure.

On the other hand, a **private cloud** is dedicated to a single organization. All cloud resources are exclusively used by that organization, giving it full control over data management, customization, and security policies. Private clouds generally offer higher flexibility and meet strict regulatory requirements more easily compared to public clouds.

Community and Hybrid Clouds

A **community cloud** is designed for use by multiple organizations that share similar requirements or objectives. These organizations may belong to the same industry sector or collaborate on joint projects, such as academic research or government operations. The resources are collectively used and sometimes jointly managed.

A **hybrid cloud** integrates two or more cloud environments (public, private, or community). Large enterprises commonly adopt this model because it allows strategic distribution of data. Typically, critical or confidential information is stored in a private cloud, while less sensitive data or services are placed in a public cloud. This combination offers both security and cost-efficiency.

IoT Enabling Technologies: Big Data Analytics

Big Data refers to massive and complex datasets generated from diverse sources such as sensors, social media, transaction systems, and smart devices. Traditional database systems are often unable to store, process, or analyze such huge amounts of data effectively. Big Data is typically defined using **six major characteristics (6Vs):**

- **Volume:** Represents the extremely large amount of data produced continuously from various devices and platforms.
- **Variety:** Indicates that data exists in multiple formats, including structured (tables), semi-structured (XML/JSON), and unstructured (audio, video, text).
- **Velocity:** Describes the rapid rate at which new data is generated and needs to be processed. Data production is now occurring in petabytes per minute in some domains.
- **Veracity:** Refers to the reliability and accuracy of the data. Incorrect, incomplete, or manipulated data leads to misleading insights and poor decision-making.
- **Value:** Focuses on extracting meaningful benefits from data. If data does not contribute to useful outcomes or revenue generation, it holds little importance.
- **Variability:** Points to the dynamic nature of data formats and usage patterns, requiring flexible processing methods.

Big Data Analytics Framework

To transform raw data into meaningful insights, Big Data analytics follows a structured workflow consisting of the following stages:

1. **Collection:** Gathering data from various sources such as sensors, servers, and web platforms.

2. **Cleaning:** Removing duplicate, incorrect, or irrelevant data.

3. **Integration:** Combining data from multiple sources into a common format.

4. **Analysis:** Applying algorithms, statistical techniques, or AI methods to extract meaningful patterns.

5. **Visualization:** Presenting results using graphs, dashboards, and reports for easy understanding.

6. **Alerting:** Generating notifications or taking automated actions based on analytical outcomes.

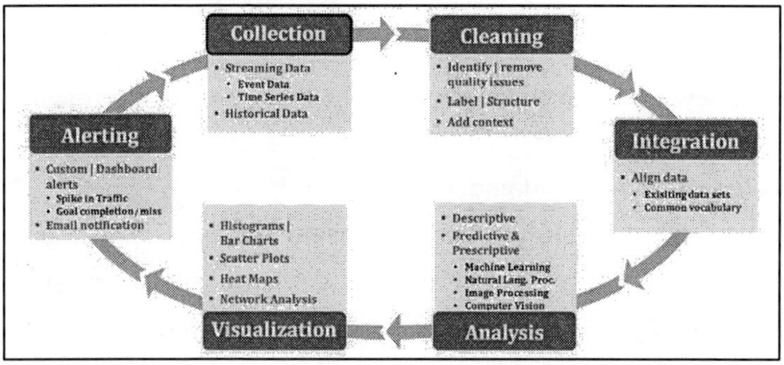

Fig. 1.21 Data Analytics Framework

IoT Enabling Technologies: Communication Protocols

Communication protocols are essential for the functioning of IoT systems because they enable devices to exchange data reliably. These protocols specify how information is formatted, encoded, addressed, and transmitted between devices. They also provide mechanisms for managing data flow, detecting errors, and ensuring secure and efficient communication. Without these protocols, connected devices would not be able to share information or coordinate actions.

IoT Enabling Technologies: Embedded Systems

An **embedded system** refers to a dedicated computing unit that is integrated with hardware to perform specific, predefined tasks. It may operate independently or as part of a larger intelligent system. Embedded systems are typically built around microprocessors or microcontrollers and consist of memory, input/output interfaces, storage units, and networking components. They generally run on **Real-Time Operating Systems (RTOS)**, which control the timing and execution of critical operations.

Core Components of an Embedded System

- **Hardware:** Includes processors, sensors, actuators, and electronic interfaces.
- **Software:** Embedded programs designed to execute particular functions.
- **RTOS:** Manages task scheduling and ensures timely execution of processes in real-time environments.

Characteristics of Embedded Systems

- Designed to perform **a single dedicated function**
- Operate under strict constraints such as memory, power, and computation
- Work in **real-time**, reacting immediately to external inputs
- Often connected to a communication network
- Have optimized memory and processing usage

1.7 Complex Interdependence of IOT Technologies

Table 1.2

Step	Technology	Role	Depends On
1	Embedded Systems	Collect physical data / Perform actions	Communication Protocols
2	Wireless Sensor Networks	Share data across connected nodes	Embedded Systems
3	Communication Protocols	Secure and manage data transfer	WSN and Cloud

4	Cloud Computing	Store, analyze, and process large-scale data	Communication Protocols
5	Big Data Analytics	Extract insights and predictions	Cloud Computing

Real-World Example: Smart Agriculture

1. Embedded devices measure soil moisture, humidity, and temperature.

2. A wireless sensor network links all sensing units across the farm.

3. Communication protocols (e.g., MQTT, Zigbee) transmit this information securely to cloud servers.

4. Cloud computing stores, monitors, and processes the data.

5. Big Data analytics predicts irrigation schedules and sends signals back to embedded systems to activate watering systems automatically.

1.8 IOT Networking Components

The core building blocks of any IoT system are:

1. Sensors/Devices

These collect real-world data such as temperature, motion, humidity, and location. Some devices can also act and control physical systems (e.g., smart locks, thermostats).

2. Connectivity

Devices communicate with each other and with cloud servers using networks such as Wi-Fi, Bluetooth, Zigbee, 4G/5G, LoRaWAN, and MQTT.

3. Data Processing / Cloud Computing

After data reaches the cloud, it is processed, stored, and analyzed. This enables real-time decision-making and automation.

4. User Interface (UI)

Users interact with IoT systems through dashboards, mobile apps, or web platforms to monitor, control, and visualize data.

5. Big Data Analytics & AI

Advanced analytics and machine learning derive insights from massive datasets to predict events, optimize performance, and support automation.

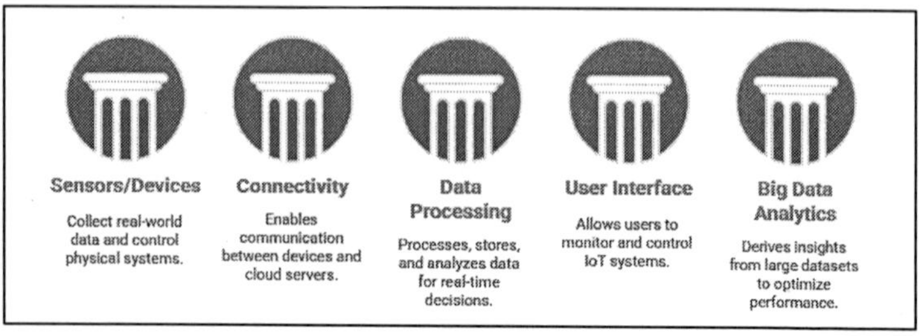

Fig. 1.22 Components of IOT

We often hear the term *Internet of Things (IoT)* in our everyday life. Simply put, IoT refers to a smart ecosystem where different devices and objects are connected to the internet, allowing them to communicate, work automatically, and be controlled remotely. This connectivity helps devices perform tasks more efficiently without direct human intervention.

Major Components of the Internet of Things

1. Smart Devices and Sensors – Device Connectivity Layer

Smart devices and sensors form the foundation of an IoT network. They continuously observe their surroundings, gather useful information, and send this data to the backend system or cloud for processing.

With advancements in semiconductor technology, compact and highly efficient micro-sensors are now widely used across multiple industries. These sensors detect everything from environmental changes to object movement and send that information forward in real time.

Common Types of IoT Sensors

- Temperature sensors and smart thermostats
- Pressure sensors

- Humidity and moisture detection sensors
- Light intensity/illumination sensors
- Soil moisture sensors
- Proximity and motion detectors
- RFID (Radio Frequency Identification) tags for tracking objects

Device-to-Device Communication Process

Smart devices communicate using low-power wireless networks. Depending on the application, range, energy consumption, and required data speed, different technologies may be used.

Popular IoT Wireless Communication Technologies

- **Wi-Fi** – High data rate, suitable for home automation
- **ZigBee** – Low energy usage, ideal for sensor networks
- **Bluetooth** – Short-range connectivity for wearables
- **Z-Wave** – Used in smart home devices due to low interference
- **LoRaWAN** – Long-range, low-power communication for smart cities and agriculture

Each of these technologies varies in battery consumption, speed, range, and reliability, making them suitable for different IoT applications. Advancements in **low-power and cost-effective wireless communication devices** are driving significant progress in the Internet of Things (IoT). These devices are designed to operate efficiently for long periods on minimal battery power, making them ideal for remote and scalable IoT applications. To achieve energy-efficient networking, many organizations are turning to modern communication standards such as **6LoWPAN (IPv6 over Low Power Wireless Personal Area Networks)**. This protocol enables small, low-energy devices to communicate using IPv6, ensuring secure and scalable connections without draining battery resources. One of the key advantages of 6LoWPAN is its ability to **minimize transmission duration**. It sends data in **short bursts or pulses**, which reduces energy consumption and significantly extends device life. As a result, even battery-operated sensors can function reliably for years in an IoT environment.

2. Gateway

An **IoT Gateway** plays a crucial role in connecting devices and networks within an IoT ecosystem. It acts as a communication bridge that handles **two-way data flow** between different sensors, devices, and cloud platforms. One of its key responsibilities is to **translate various communication protocols**, ensuring that devices built on different technologies can work together without issues.

Gateways are also capable of performing **local data processing**. Instead of sending raw data directly to the cloud, they can filter, analyze, or compress the information generated by thousands of sensors. This local pre-processing is particularly useful when data cannot be directly transmitted using standard TCP/IP protocols or when bandwidth needs to be optimized.

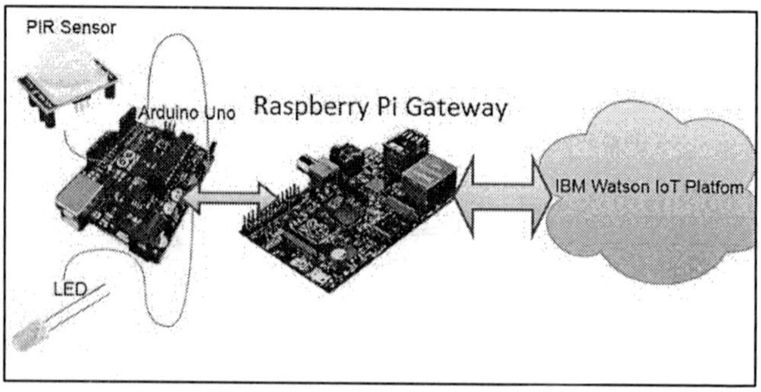

Fig. 1.23 Gateway

In addition to communication and processing, IoT gateways enhance the **security of the entire network**. They apply strong encryption and authentication mechanisms to safeguard data transfer and prevent unauthorized access. By serving as a protective layer between edge devices and the cloud, gateways help shield IoT systems from cyber threats and malicious attacks.

3. Cloud

The **Internet of Things (IoT)** generates an enormous volume of data from connected sensors, applications, and users. To handle this information effectively, organizations rely on the **IoT cloud**, which provides advanced tools for collecting, storing, managing, and analyzing data in real time. Through cloud platforms, industries can remotely access device data and make informed decisions without needing to be physically present at the location of the system.

In simple terms, the IoT cloud is a **powerful infrastructure made up of high-speed servers** designed to support billions of connected devices. These servers enable rapid data processing, manage heavy network traffic, and deliver precise analytical results. A key part of this ecosystem is the **distributed database system**, which ensures that massive data sets can be stored and accessed efficiently from multiple locations.

Cloud platforms bring together a wide range of elements—devices, sensors, gateways, communication protocols, and large storage systems—and use them to generate **predictive analytics**. Businesses rely on these insights to improve their products, enhance services, plan preventive measures, reduce operational costs, and design new business strategies with higher accuracy.

4. Analytics

Analytics plays a key role in IoT by transforming raw, unstructured data gathered from billions of connected sensors and devices into meaningful insights. These insights can then be interpreted, monitored, and used to optimize the overall functioning of IoT systems. Without efficient data analytics, managing and improving large IoT ecosystems would be almost impossible.

A major benefit of IoT is its ability to deliver **real-time analytics**, enabling engineers and system operators to immediately detect abnormal patterns or faults in the incoming data. Quick identification of such irregularities allows experts to respond promptly and prevent failures, security threats, or unexpected disruptions. When accurate data is captured at the right moment, service providers can make timely decisions and plan future actions effectively.

Large organizations rely on the vast amount of data produced by IoT solutions to explore new business opportunities. With careful and structured analysis, companies can forecast market demands, understand user behavior, and develop strategies to stay competitive. Since reliable information drives better outcomes, **predictive analytics becomes a vital tool** for shaping successful business models and ensuring long-term growth.

5. User interface

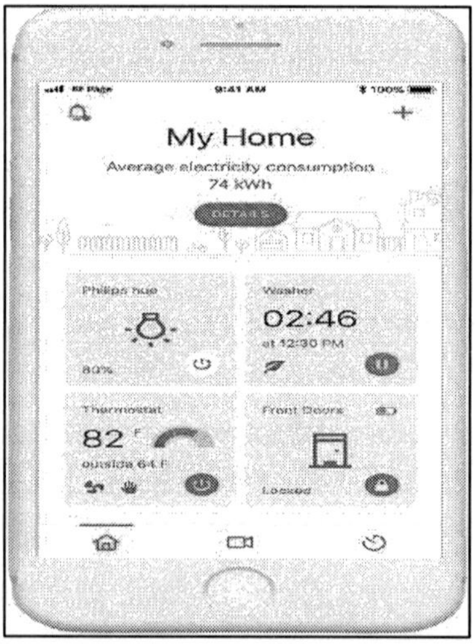

Fig. 1.24 Gateway

User Interfaces in IoT

- **User Interfaces (UI)** represent the **visible and interactive part** of an IoT system through which users operate devices and access data.
- A well-designed UI should:
  - Require **minimum effort** from users.

  - **Encourage more interaction** through ease of use.

- Modern technology enables highly interactive UIs using **touch panels, multicolor displays, and smart controls**, replacing traditional physical switches.
- In today's market, UI design has become a **major deciding factor for customers** when choosing smart devices, especially those compatible with common **wireless standards**.

1.9 Introduction to IOT Sensing

- **Sensors** are fundamental components of IoT used to **sense physical parameters** like temperature, humidity, pressure, motion, etc.
- They **detect physical quantities** and convert them into **usable signals** (electrical, mechanical, or optical).
- The output signal is further **processed and converted** into a **human-readable format**, such as changes in:
  - Resistance
  - Capacitance
  - Impedance
  - Any other measurable characteristic

Smart Analytics in IoT (Previous Paragraph Summary)

- IoT analytics converts **massive analog data from billions of devices** into meaningful insights.
- **Real-time analytics** helps detect irregularities and take fast preventive actions.
- Enterprises use IoT data to **plan business strategies, forecast market trends, and make predictive decisions**, improving overall success.

IoT Hardware

Transducer

A **transducer** is a device that converts one form of energy into another.

It receives a physical quantity (such as temperature, pressure, sound, or light) and transforms it into an electrical signal or vice versa. In many IoT systems, transducers may also act as **actuators**, performing actions based on electrical input.

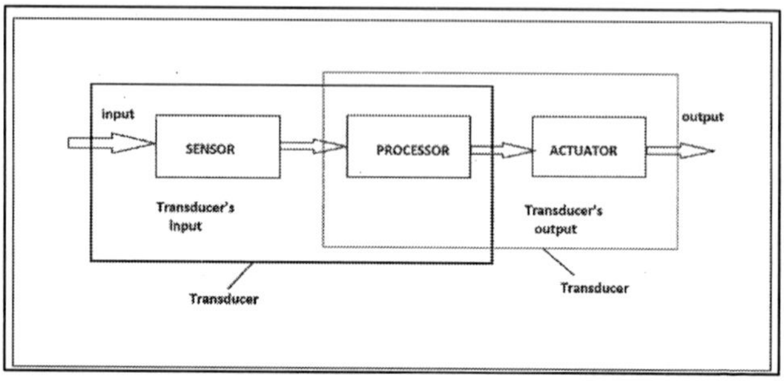

Fig. 1.25 IOT Hardware

1.10 Types of Sensors

1. Electrical Sensors

Electrical proximity sensors may work with contact or without contact:

- **Contact sensors** operate by physically completing an electrical circuit.
- **Non-contact sensors** use:
  - **Inductive principles** for detecting metals.
  - **Capacitive principles** for detecting non-metals.

2. Light Sensors

Light sensors (or photosensors) detect changes in light intensity. A commonly used light sensor is the **Light Dependent Resistor (LDR)**.

Property:

The resistance of an LDR is **inversely proportional** to the light intensity.

- More light → lower resistance
- Less light → higher resistance

3. Touch Sensors

Touch sensors detect the **presence or touch** of a finger or stylus.

Types of Touch Sensors

1. **Resistive**
2. **Capacitive**

Modern devices primarily use **capacitive touch sensors** due to higher accuracy and better noise immunity.

4. Range Sensors

Range or distance sensors determine how **far or near** an object is from the sensor.

- **Short-range sensing** (few mm to a few hundred mm): Uses capacitance, inductance, or magnetic methods.
- **Long-range sensing**: Uses transmitted energy such as **radio waves, ultrasonic waves, or laser beams**.

5. Mechanical Sensors

Mechanical sensors use physical switches to detect movement or contact.

Because they require applied force to operate, **micro-switches** are commonly used.

6. Pneumatic Sensors

These sensors work by **interrupting or disturbing airflow**. They are contact-type sensors and are unsuitable where light components may be displaced by air.

7. Optical Sensors

Optical sensors detect objects by **blocking or reflecting light** onto a light-sensitive device like a photocell.

They are **non-contact sensors**, but environmental conditions such as dust, smoke, or bright flashes (e.g., welding) can interfere with their performance.

8. Speed Sensors

Speed sensors measure the **speed of a moving object or vehicle**. **Examples:**

- Wind speed sensors
- Speedometers

- Doppler radar (UDAR)
- Ground speed radar

9. Temperature Sensors

Temperature sensors measure temperature and convert it into an **electrical signal**. The output voltage is **directly proportional** to temperature.

10. PIR Sensor (Passive Infrared Sensor)

PIR sensors detect **infrared radiation** emitted by warm objects. They are widely used for **motion detection** and **human presence detection**.

11. Ultrasonic Sensors

Ultrasonic sensors operate on the same principle as **SONAR and RADAR**.

They emit high-frequency sound waves and analyze the echo to determine the **distance and shape** of a target.

1.11 Sensor Characteristics

Sensor characteristics are broadly classified into:

1. **Static Characteristics**
2. **Dynamic Characteristics**

1. Static Characteristics

Static characteristics describe how a sensor behaves when measuring a quantity under steady-state conditions (i.e., when the input does not change rapidly).

• **Accuracy**

Accuracy indicates how close the sensor's measured value is to the actual (true) value of the quantity. It represents the error in measurement and is evaluated using:

- **Absolute Error:** Absolute Error = Measured Value – True Value
- **Relative Error:** Relative Error = Measured Value / True Value

A highly accurate sensor produces outputs very close to the true value.

- **Range**

The **range** defines the minimum and maximum values of the quantity that a sensor can reliably detect. Outside this interval, the sensor cannot provide a meaningful output. **Example:** An RTD temperature sensor typically works from **–200°C to 800°C**.

- **Resolution**

Resolution refers to the smallest change in input that a sensor can detect. A sensor with high resolution can sense very tiny variations. When the smallest input change that can be detected is zero, this point is known as the **threshold**.

- **Precision**

Precision describes the ability of a sensor to give consistent readings when the same quantity is measured repeatedly under identical conditions. It is related to the **repeatability** and **variance** of measurements. Precision does **not** indicate closeness to the true value—only consistency.

- **Sensitivity**

Sensitivity expresses how much the sensor output changes in response to a change in input. It is usually represented by the **slope of the output-input graph**. High sensitivity means even a small input change produces a noticeable output change.

- **Linearity**

Linearity shows how close the sensor's output curve is to a straight line. If the output increases proportionally with the input, the sensor is said to be **highly linear**. Calibration curves (output vs. input under static conditions) are used to assess linearity.

- **Drift**

Drift is the gradual change in the sensor output when the input remains constant for a long duration. It reduces accuracy over time and requires recalibration.

- **Repeatability**

Repeatability is the ability of a sensor to produce the same output when the same input is applied repeatedly within a short time span.

It ensures consistent performance without influence from long-term drift.

2. Dynamic Characteristics

Dynamic characteristics describe how a sensor responds when the input changes with time.

• **Zero-Order System**

- The output follows the input instantly with **no time delay**.
- Contains no energy storage elements. **Example:** Potentiometers used for measuring linear or rotational displacement.

• **First-Order System**

- The output changes gradually and takes some time to reach the final steady value.
- Includes one energy-storing and one energy-dissipating component.

• **Second-Order System**

- Produces a more complex response.
- Output may **oscillate** before settling at a steady-state value.
- Common in sensors where mechanical or electrical resonance occurs.

Sensor Classification

Sensors can be classified into several categories depending on how they operate and what type of data they generate.

1. Passive and Active Sensors

• **Passive Sensors**

Passive sensors **cannot generate their own signal**. They rely entirely on external input energy to operate. **Examples:** Accelerometers, soil-moisture sensors, water-level sensors, temperature sensors.

• **Active Sensors**

Active sensors **generate their own excitation signal** and sense the response from the environment. **Examples:** Radar systems, laser altimeters, sounder sensors.

2. Analog and Digital Sensors

- **Analog Sensors**

These sensors produce a **continuous output** corresponding to the input quantity.

The signal varies smoothly and has infinite possible values. **Examples:** LDR, temperature sensors, analog pressure sensors, analog Hall-effect sensors.

- **Digital Sensors**

Digital sensors provide output in **binary form (0 or 1)**. They include an internal analog-to-digital conversion circuit to overcome analog limitations. **Examples:** PIR sensor, digital temperature sensor (DS1620).

3. Scalar and Vector Sensors

- **Scalar Sensors**

Scalar sensors measure quantities that have **only magnitude**, not direction.

Their output depends solely on how much of a parameter is present. **Examples:** Temperature sensors, gas detectors, smoke sensors, strain sensors, color sensors.

- **Vector Sensors**

Vector sensors measure quantities that have **both magnitude and direction**.

Their output changes when the orientation of the input changes. **Examples:** Accelerometers, gyroscopes, magnetic field sensors, motion detectors.

1.12 Sensorial Deviation in IoT

Sensorial deviation refers to any difference between the actual value of a physical quantity and the value reported by a sensor. These deviations represent **errors, inaccuracies, or distortions** in sensor data. Since IoT systems rely heavily on accurate data, minimizing such deviations is essential for reliable decision-making and system performance.

Types of Sensorial Deviations

1. Sensor Drift

A slow, long-term shift in a sensor's output that occurs even when the measured property remains constant. Drift can result from environmental effects, component aging, or mechanical stress.

2. Offset Error (Bias)

A constant error where the sensor readings are consistently above or below the true value by a fixed amount. This type of deviation usually occurs due to incorrect initial calibration or manufacturing imperfections.

3. Gain Error

A proportional error that affects the **slope or sensitivity** of the sensor. For example, a temperature sensor may be accurate at lower values but progressively inaccurate at higher temperatures due to wrong scaling.

4. Non-Linearity

When the sensor output does not follow the ideal straight-line relationship between input and output. Many sensors are designed for linear response, and deviations from linearity reduce measurement accuracy.

5. Hysteresis Error

This occurs when the output value depends on the direction of the input change.

A sensor may give one reading when a parameter is increasing and a different one when the same parameter is decreasing.

6. Noise

Random fluctuations or spikes in the sensor output. While noise is unavoidable, it is typically removed through filtering and signal processing techniques.

7. Quantization Error

Occurs in digital sensors during the **analog-to-digital conversion** process.

Since digital systems store data in discrete values, the original analog signal gets approximated, causing small errors.

Causes of Sensorial Deviations

- **Environmental Influences**

Factors like temperature, humidity, pressure, and vibrations can alter sensor performance. Many semiconductor sensors are especially sensitive to ambient temperature changes.

- **Aging and Wear**

Over time, sensor materials degrade, mechanical parts loosen, or circuits weaken, leading to drift and increased errors.

- **Manufacturing Defects**

Production flaws can result in initial measurement biases or inconsistent sensor behavior right from the start.

- **Changes in Data Collection Techniques**

Altering the sampling rate, data filtering methods, or installation conditions may introduce new sources of error.

- **External Interference**

Electromagnetic fields from motors, welding equipment, or nearby electrical devices can introduce unwanted noise into sensor signals.

Managing Sensorial Deviations in IoT

To ensure dependable sensor data, IoT systems use several strategies and techniques:

1. Calibration

Comparing sensor outputs with a reference standard and adjusting them to correct deviations. Calibration may be done manually, during manufacturing, or automatically using software algorithms.

2. Drift Compensation

Statistical models and machine learning techniques predict drift trends and adjust the readings accordingly. This reduces the need for frequent manual recalibration.

3. Anomaly Detection

Machine learning algorithms continuously monitor sensor data to flag abnormal patterns that may indicate sensor failure or data corruption. This is especially useful in large-scale IoT deployments like smart factories or predictive maintenance systems.

4. Redundancy and Sensor Fusion

Using multiple sensors to measure the same parameter helps cross-check data. Data fusion techniques combine readings to generate more accurate and trustworthy measurements.

5. Edge Computing

Processing data close to the source (on the device or local gateway) allows real-time filtering, noise reduction, normalization, and early detection of outliers. This reduces the amount of inaccurate data reaching the cloud.

6. MLOps (Machine Learning Operations)

Maintaining and updating ML models to ensure they adapt to changes in sensor behavior over time. MLOps helps prevent model degradation caused by sensor drift or data shifts.

1.13 Sensing Considerations in IoT

Selecting the right sensor for an IoT system requires evaluating several key factors. These include technical performance, environmental durability, power consumption, connectivity, cost, security, and the ability to scale. A well-selected sensor ensures reliable, accurate, and long-term data collection that supports the overall goals of the IoT application.

1. Technical and Performance Factors

These characteristics determine how accurately and consistently a sensor can measure a physical quantity.

• **Accuracy**

Indicates how close a sensor's reading is to the true or actual value. High-accuracy sensors are essential in applications where even small errors are unacceptable—such as medical devices or industrial quality control.

- **Precision / Repeatability**

Refers to how consistently a sensor produces the same output when measuring the same input under the same conditions.

- **Sensitivity**

Defines how much the sensor's output changes for a small change in the measured parameter. Higher sensitivity allows the detection of finer variations.

- **Range**

Specifies the minimum and maximum limits within which a sensor can measure accurately. A sensor with an appropriate range ensures both reliable readings and longer lifespan.

- **Resolution**

The smallest measurable change the sensor can detect. Higher resolution provides more detailed and fine-grained data.

- **Response Time**

The time taken by the sensor to react to changes in the physical quantity. Real-time applications—like automated control systems—require sensors with fast response times.

- **Linearity**

Describes how closely the sensor's output follows a straight-line relationship with the input. Good linearity simplifies data analysis and calibration.

- **Drift**

A gradual shift in sensor output over time unrelated to actual changes in the measured value. Low drift is important for long-term deployments.

2. Environmental and Operational Factors

These factors determine if the sensor can survive and function effectively in its intended environment.

- **Operating Environment**

The sensor must withstand the environmental conditions where it will be deployed—temperature, humidity, dust, chemicals, or vibrations. Industrial applications often require rugged or weather-proof sensors.

• **Form Factor and Size**

Compact sensors are crucial for space-limited applications such as wearables, drones, or embedded devices. Ease of mounting and integration also matters.

• **Power Efficiency**

Low power consumption is critical for battery-driven or remote IoT devices.

Techniques like duty cycling, sleep modes, energy harvesting, and low-power communication protocols help extend battery life.

• **Communication Protocols**

Sensors must support suitable connectivity standards based on application requirements:

- **BLE** for short-range, low-power communication
- **LoRaWAN / NB-IoT** for long-range, low-power needs
- **Wi-Fi / Cellular** for high-bandwidth or real-time applications

3. Cost and Scalability

Financial and organizational factors heavily influence sensor selection.

• **Cost vs. Return on Investment (ROI)**

The final choice should balance initial sensor costs with long-term benefits such as improved productivity, safety, or reduced downtime.

• **Scalability**

The system should support adding more sensors over time without major redesign. This includes handling larger data volumes and ensuring smooth integration.

• **Maintenance and Calibration**

Some sensors require regular calibration to maintain accuracy. Choosing sensors that are easy to maintain reduces downtime and long-term operational costs.

4. Data Management and Security

IoT systems generate large amounts of data, and protecting this data is critical.

• **Data Output and Compatibility**

Consider whether the sensor outputs analog or digital data and ensure compatibility with existing hardware, microcontrollers, and communication systems.

• **Data Security**

Sensors must not expose the IoT network to vulnerabilities. Strong encryption, secure communication protocols, authentication, and adherence to privacy standards help protect data from cyber threats.

1.14 Introduction to Actuators

An IoT (Internet of Things) device typically consists of five main components:

a physical object (thing), a controller or processor, sensors, actuators, and a communication network. Among these, **actuators** play the role of performing physical actions in the real world.

Basics of Actuator Technology

An **actuator** is a device or machine component that **converts electrical signals into physical motion**. It performs the action required by the IoT system based on instructions from the controller.

- Sensors **collect data** from the environment.
- The controller **analyzes** this data and decides what needs to be done.
- Actuators then **execute the action** (move, rotate, open, close, push, pull, etc.).

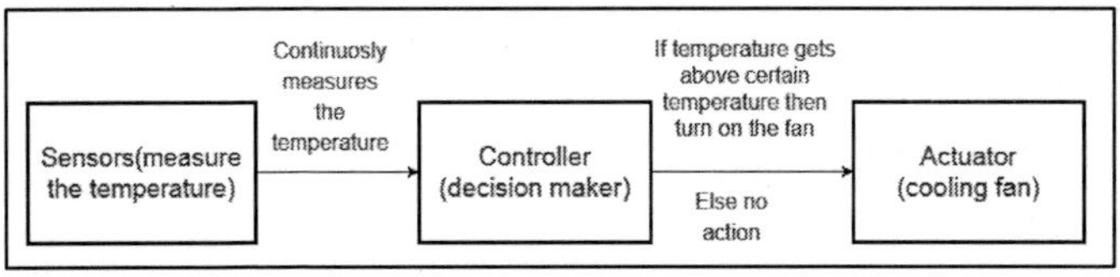

Fig. 1.26 Working of IoT Devices and Use of Actuators

An IoT device typically includes **sensors, a controller, actuators, and a communication network**. Sensors observe the environment, the controller makes decisions, and actuators carry out the required physical action.

Working Mechanism of IoT Systems Integrated with Actuators

In an IoT system:

1. **Sensors detect environmental conditions** (temperature, pressure, motion, humidity, etc.)
2. **Controller processes the sensor data** using a microcontroller or processor (Arduino, ESP32, Raspberry Pi).
3. **Controller sends a control signal to an actuator** based on the required response.
4. **Actuator converts the control signal + energy source into physical motion or action** (moving, pushing, rotating, heating, etc.).

Thus, the actuator is the component that **interacts with the physical world**, enabling automation in IoT applications.

1.15 Actuator Types

1. Hydraulic Actuators

Use **pressurized hydraulic fluid** to generate rotary, linear, or oscillatory motion. Commonly used where **high force** is needed.

Examples

- Construction machinery
- Vehicle lifting systems
- Heavy robotics

Advantages

- Produces **high force** and high speed
- Ideal for heavy-duty applications
- Used in welding, clamping, lifting

Disadvantages

- Hydraulic fluid leakage → maintenance issues
- Noisy and expensive

- Needs regular cleaning, heat exchangers, and noise reduction systems

2. Pneumatic Actuators

Use **compressed air or vacuum pressure** to produce motion.

Examples

- Robotic grippers
- Packaging machines
- Air-powered tools

Advantages

- Low-cost option
- Safe for extreme temperatures
- Quick start/stop response
- Low maintenance and durable

Disadvantages

- Pressure loss reduces efficiency
- Air compressor must run continuously
- Air contamination leads to maintenance issues

3. Electrical Actuators

Use **electric motors** to convert electrical energy into mechanical torque.

Examples

- Solenoid valves
- Electric bells
- Smart home appliances
- Servo and stepper motors

Advantages

- Clean, quiet, and safe (no fluids)
- Highly precise and programmable
- Ideal for automation

Disadvantages

- Expensive compared to pneumatic actuators
- Sensitive to environmental conditions (heat, moisture)

Other Types of Actuators

4. Thermal / Magnetic Actuators

Use **thermal energy or magnetic energy**.

Examples:

- Shape Memory Alloys (SMA)
- Magnetic Shape Memory Alloys (MSMA)
- Piezo motors

5. Mechanical Actuators

Convert **rotary motion to linear motion** using gears, pulleys, or cams. Example: **Crankshaft** in engines.

6. Soft Actuators

Made of flexible materials, used in:

- Soft robotics
- Wearable devices
- Artificial muscles

7. Shape Memory Polymers

Change shape when heated or exposed to stimuli.

8. Light-Activated Polymers

Respond to light for motion—used in smart materials and biomedical applications.

1.16 Actuator Characteristics

1. Energy Conversion

Actuators convert electrical control signals into **mechanical movement, heat, sound, or light**. Example: In a smart thermostat, the actuator converts an electrical signal into a mechanical action to turn ON/OFF heating.

2. Physical Interaction

Actuators directly perform physical tasks such as:

- Moving a robotic arm
- Opening/closing a valve
- Rotating a motor

- Switching ON a light

3. Dependence on Control Signals

Actuators only operate when they receive commands from a controller. The controller analyses the sensor data and instructs the actuator.

4. Feedback Capability

Advanced actuators provide feedback to the controller about task completion.

This **closed-loop control** improves accuracy and reliability.

5. Types of Motion

- **Linear Motion** → Sliding doors, conveyors
- **Rotary Motion** → Fans, servo motors, robotic joints

Critical Requirements of Actuators for IoT Applications

1. Precision and Accuracy

Used in robotics, medical devices, and automation where exact movement is essential.

2. Low Power Consumption

IoT devices often run on batteries; therefore, actuators must be energy-efficient.

3. Compact Size and Lightweight

Wearables and portable devices require small actuators.

4. Durability and Ruggedness

Industrial IoT requires actuators that can resist: Heat, dust, pressure, corrosion, moisture.

5. Cost-Effectiveness

Affordable actuators improve widespread adoption of IoT systems.

6. Connectivity and Interoperability

Actuators must support IoT communication protocols such as: **Wi-Fi, Bluetooth, Zigbee, LoRa, MQTT**, etc.

Difference Between Sensor and Actuator

Sensors and actuators are two essential components of an IoT system, but they perform opposite roles. A **sensor** detects changes in the environment, while an **actuator** performs an action based on control signals.

Table 1.3

Parameters	Sensor	Actuator
Basics	Sensors convert the physical characteristics from their environment to electrical signals for the system.	Actuators convert the electrical signals from the system to various physical characteristics for their environments.
Source of Input	Sensors receive input from their environments.	Actuators receive input from a system's output conditioning unit.
Output Generation	Sensors generate output for a system's input conditioning unit.	These generate output for their environment.
Type of Output	Electrical signals are generated as output by sensors.	Motion or heat is generated as output by actuators.
Placement	Sensors are placed at a system's input port.	Actuators are placed at a system's output port.
Examples	For instance, thermometers take our body temperatures in the form of physical characteristics, convert the temperatures into electrical	For instance, heaters, comb drives, pneumatic cylinders, hydraulic cylinders, and

	signals, and convey them to their systems. Photo-voltaic cells, Tilt sensors, Temperature sensors, Accelerometers, Ultrasonic sensors, etc., are a few types of sensors.	electric motors are some of the common actuators you can find around you.

Exercise

A. Objective Questions (MCQs)

1. A group of interconnected devices that share data and resources is called a:

a) Database

b) Network

c) Server

d) Protocol

Answer: b) Network

2. LAN is generally used for:

a) Long-distance communication

b) A small geographical area

c) Satellite links

d) High-speed global networks

Answer: b) A small geographical area

3. Which layer of the OSI model provides end-to-end delivery?

a) Application

b) Transport

c) Network

d) Session

Answer: b) Transport

4. TCP/IP model consists of how many layers?

a) 2

b) 4

c) 6

d) 7

Answer: b) 4

5. IoT means:

a) Information of Technology

b) Interconnection of Tools

c) Internet of Things

d) Intelligent Online Transfer

Answer: c) Internet of Things

6. Which of the following contributed to the rapid growth of IoT?

a) Cloud computing

b) Low-cost sensors

c) Wireless communication

d) All of the above

Answer: d) All of the above

7. A device that connects IoT sensors to a network is known as a:

a) Relay

b) Gateway

c) Antenna

d) Transistor

Answer: b) Gateway

8. A sensor is a device that:

a) Stores data

b) Executes commands

c) Measures physical parameters

d) Displays output

Answer: c) Measures physical parameters

9. Which of the following is a type of actuator?

a) LDR

b) Thermistor

c) DC Motor

d) Photodiode

Answer: c) DC Motor

10. Sensor drift is related to:

a) Sensor failure

b) Measurement deviation over time

c) Noise removal

d) Incorrect wiring

Answer: b) Measurement deviation over time

B. Very Short Answer Questions (1–2 marks)

Basics of Networking

1. Define a computer network.
2. What is meant by network topology?
3. What is a layered network model?
4. Give two examples of network types.

Emergence of IoT

5. Define IoT in simple words.
6. Mention two major enabling technologies of IoT.
7. What do you mean by IoT evolution?
8. What is an IoT gateway?

IoT Sensing and Actuation

9. What is a sensor?
10. What are actuator devices?
11. Define sensor accuracy.
12. What are sensorial deviations?
13. Give two examples of sensing types.
14. What is meant by an actuator's response time?

C. Short Answer Questions (3–5 marks)

Basics of Networking

1. Explain the different types of computer networks with examples.
2. Why is layered architecture used in networking?
3. Write a short note on the OSI model.

Emergence of IoT

4. Describe the key stages in the evolution of IoT.

5. Explain how various technologies work together to enable IoT.

6. List and explain important IoT networking components.

IoT Sensing & Actuation

7. Discuss any four important characteristics of sensors.

8. What are the major types of sensor deviations? Explain with examples.

9. Explain different sensing types used in IoT applications.

10. Write short notes on:

(a) Actuator types

(b) Sensing considerations

11. How do sensors and actuators complement each other in IoT?

D. Long Answer Questions (8–10 marks)

Basics of Networking

1. Explain the concept of computer networking. Describe different network types such as LAN, MAN, and WAN with suitable diagrams.

2. Discuss the layered network models in detail. Compare the OSI and TCP/IP models with their features and functions.

Emergence of IoT

3. Describe the emergence and evolution of IoT. Highlight the technological trends that led to its development.

4. Explain the enabling technologies behind IoT and describe how these technologies depend on each other.

5. Provide a detailed explanation of IoT networking components and their roles in data flow from sensors to cloud platforms.

IoT Sensing & Actuation

6. Define sensors and actuators. Describe their characteristics, classifications, and importance in IoT systems.

7. Explain sensor characteristics and sensorial deviations in detail. Discuss how deviations affect IoT system accuracy and reliability.

8. Describe different sensing types and sensing considerations, with examples from real-world IoT applications.

9. Discuss actuator types and characteristics. Explain how actuators are selected for IoT-based automation systems.

10. Explain the complete sensing–processing–actuation cycle in IoT devices with a neat diagram and suitable examples.

Unit-2

IoT Processing Topologies and Types

2.1 Data Formats in IOT

A **data format** specifies the structure and organization of data, making it understandable and usable for machines and software systems. It determines how information is stored, displayed, and exchanged between devices.

Choosing an appropriate data format depends on several factors, such as:

- **Device capabilities:** available processing power, memory, and storage.
- **Network limitations:** how much bandwidth is available for data transmission.
- **Size of the data:** the volume and frequency of information being transferred.
- **Application needs:** requirements for speed, ease of interpretation, compatibility, and system integration.

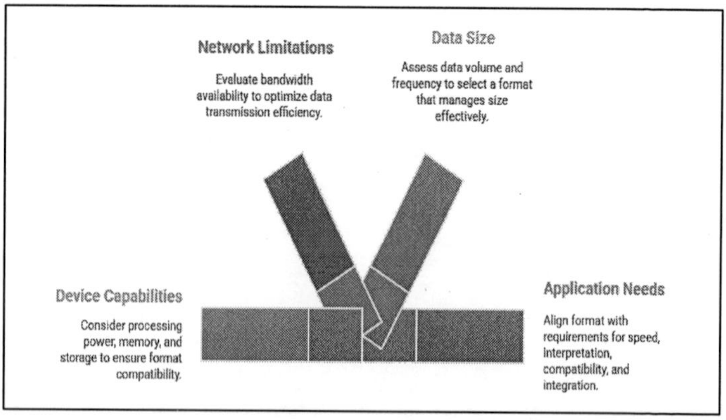

Fig 2.1 Data Format Depending Factors

Examples of common data formats include:

- **JSON** – organizes data as key–value pairs, making it easy to parse and lightweight for IoT applications.
- **XML** – represents information through hierarchical, nested tags, providing strong structure and readability.
- **CSV** – arranges data in rows and columns separated by commas, suitable for simple and large data collections.

1. Types of IoT Data

A. Structured Data

Definition:

Structured data refers to information that is neatly organized and follows a predefined format or schema. It is arranged in predictable fields—such as rows, columns, or labeled attributes—making it simple to store, query, and analyze.

Where it is stored: Such data fits well in relational databases (SQL), time-series databases, and cloud-based IoT data storage systems.

Common Examples:

- Temperature, humidity, and pressure readings from sensors
- GPS location values such as latitude and longitude
- Smart utility meter output (electricity, water, gas usage)

Sample structured data in JSON format:

```
{
  "device_id": "sensor_01",
  "temperature": 26.5,
  "humidity": 60,
  "timestamp": "2025-10-17T10:30:00Z"
}
```

Examples of structured data formats:

Table 2.1

Format	Description	Use
CSV	Comma-Separated Values	Data logging, storage
JSON	Key–value pairs (lightweight)	APIs, cloud communication
XML	Tag-based structured data	Configuration, legacy IoT systems
BSON / MessagePack / CBOR	Binary structured data	Low-power or embedded IoT devices
Protobuf / Avro	Schema-based binary data	Cloud, big data analytics

B. Unstructured Data

Definition:

Unstructured data refers to information that does *not* follow a predefined model or organized layout. It has no fixed schema, meaning it cannot be neatly arranged in tables like rows and columns. Because of its free-form nature, it typically requires preprocessing, filtering, or AI techniques before meaningful analysis can be performed.

Why it is challenging: This type of data is not directly machine-readable and often needs advanced tools such as computer vision, natural language processing (NLP), or audio processing algorithms.

Common Examples:

- Images captured by IoT surveillance or monitoring cameras
- Audio clips collected by smart speakers or security devices
- Video footage from CCTV systems
- Unstructured text logs generated by machines or network devices

Sample unstructured IoT data:

- Continuous video stream from a smart security camera
- Raw audio from a voicc-enabled IoT assistant
- Text log entries such as:
    - *"Error: Device connection lost at 10:35:22"*
    - *"Connection restored at 10:36:04"*

Examples of unstructured data formats:

Table 2.2

Format	Description	Use
MP4 / AVI	Video formats	Surveillance, smart cities
JPEG / PNG	Image formats	Object detection, vision systems
WAV / MP3	Audio formats	Voice recognition, alerts
TXT / LOG	Plain text logs	Device monitoring
Binary streams	Raw binary data	Low-level sensor communication

3. Structured vs. Unstructured Data in IoT

Table 2.3

Feature	Structured Data	Unstructured Data
Format	Organized (rows, columns, key-value)	No predefined structure
Storage	Databases (SQL, NoSQL)	File systems, object storage
Processing	Easy and fast	Requires preprocessing (AI/ML)

Example Sources	Temperature, GPS, humidity sensors	Cameras, microphones, logs
Data Formats	JSON, CSV, XML, Protobuf	MP4, JPEG, MP3, TXT

3. Real IoT Example

A **Smart Home System** may produce both structured and unstructured data:

Table 2.4

Device	Type of Data	Data Format
Thermostat	Structured (temperature, humidity)	JSON, CSV
Security Camera	Unstructured (video feed)	MP4
Voice Assistant	Unstructured (audio input)	WAV / MP3
Smart Plug	Structured (power usage, on/off)	JSON

2.2 Importance of Processing in IoT

Processing is a fundamental part of any IoT system because it converts the huge amounts of raw data generated by devices into meaningful, usable information. Without processing, IoT data would remain unorganized and difficult to interpret. Effective processing enables real-time actions, automation, better performance, and optimized resource usage—especially when using modern techniques like edge computing.

The Vital Role of Processing

- **Data Transformation**

IoT sensors generate continuous streams of raw data. Processing organizes, filters, and converts this data into useful insights that can support monitoring, prediction, and system control.

- **Real-time Decision-Making**

Many IoT applications depend on immediate responses. Quick processing enables fast decisions—for example, anti-lock braking in vehicles or smart traffic systems adjusting signals instantly.

- **Automation and Actuation**

Processed data is used by controllers to trigger actuators. This allows systems to perform automatic actions such as adjusting temperature, controlling machines, or sending alerts without human involvement.

- **Efficiency and Optimization**

By processing data locally (edge computing), only relevant or summarized data is sent to the cloud. This reduces network usage, lowers communication costs, and speeds up the system.

- **Better User Experience**

Smart responses, fast alerts, and intelligent adjustments—all made possible by data processing—enhance the overall performance and interactivity of IoT devices.

The IoT Data Processing Journey

1. **Data Collection** – Sensors gather raw information such as temperature, motion, sound, pressure, etc.
2. **Preprocessing** – The raw data is cleaned, filtered, normalized, and converted into a usable format.
3. **Analysis** – Techniques like machine learning, statistical modeling, and data analytics identify trends and insights.
4. **Decision-Making** – The system evaluates the processed data and selects an appropriate action.
5. **Action** – Actuators perform operations, alerts are generated, or recommendations are issued.
6. **Feedback Loop** – New data generated after the action helps improve the system continuously.

2.3 IoT Processing Topologies

Selecting the right processing topology is crucial when designing an IoT system. A good architecture minimizes energy usage, reduces bandwidth requirements, and improves overall system performance. There are two major processing topologies:

1. On-site Processing Topology

In this topology, data is processed **locally**, directly at the device or gateway. Since the computation happens at the source, the system responds quickly.

This approach is ideal for applications that require **very low latency** and **instant action**. Examples of IoT systems using on-site processing:

- Healthcare monitoring devices (e.g., cardiac monitors that must react immediately)
- Flight control and avionics systems
- Industrial automation (robotic arms, conveyor systems, real-time quality control)

Local processing ensures high speed, reliability, and reduced network dependency.

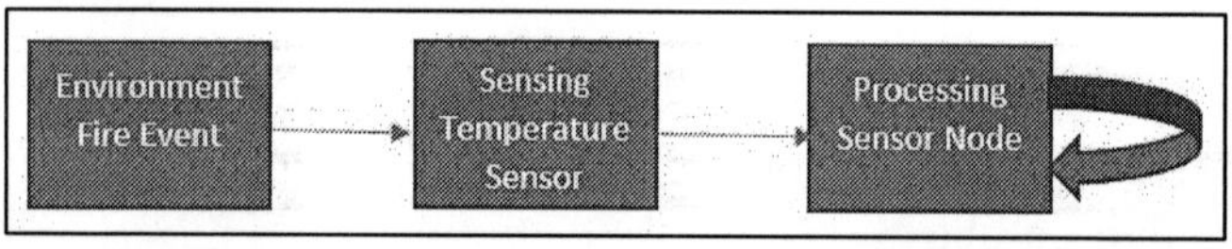

Fig. 2.2 On-site processing

2. Off-site Topology

Off-Site Topology in IoT

In an **off-site processing topology**, the data generated by IoT devices is sent to a **remote server or cloud platform** for analysis. Since the computation happens away from the device, the local hardware does not need high processing power. However, this method may introduce **latency** because data must travel over the network.

This approach is ideal for use cases where **instant results are not**

mandatory.

Examples of applications using off-site processing

- Smart agriculture monitoring and analytics
- Smart city management systems
- Large-scale environmental monitoring
- Long-term trend analysis and reporting

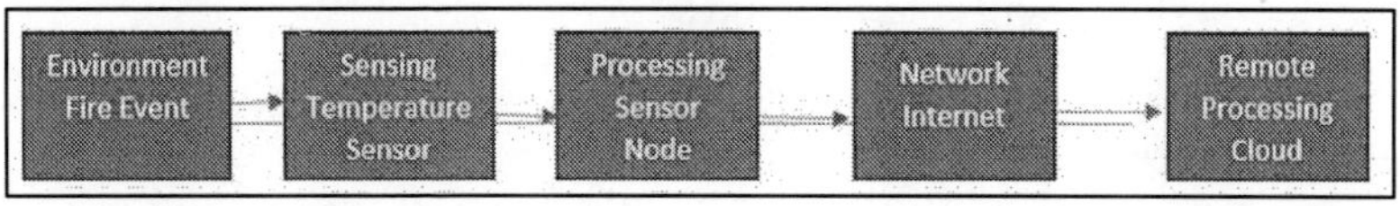

Fig. 2.3 Event detection using an off-site remote processing topology

Types of Off-Site Processing

1. Remote Processing

Also known as cloud-based processing, this is the most widely used method in IoT architecture. Data from sensor nodes is transmitted to a **central cloud or remote server**, where computation, analysis, and decision-making are performed.

Key Features

- A single high-performance server can process data from **hundreds or thousands of sensors**.
- Enables **cost savings** because resources are shared across multiple devices.
- Sensors perform basic sensing locally, while **intelligent decisions** are made remotely.
- Requires a **stable and continuous network connection**.
- High network bandwidth may be needed because data is transmitted continuously.

2. Collaborative Processing

In **collaborative processing**, data is handled by **more than one remote system or cloud platform** instead of a single server. These distributed systems work together to process data more efficiently. The workload is divided among multiple computing nodes, which helps improve speed, accuracy, and reliability in large-scale IoT applications.

Collaborative processing is used in situations where the network connection to remote servers is weak, costly, or completely unavailable. In this topology, **nearby IoT nodes work together and share their processing capabilities**, allowing data to be analyzed locally instead of sending everything to a central cloud system.

Key Features

- **Best for large, wide-area IoT deployments.** Multiple nodes across a field, factory, or region combine their processing power.
- **Local processing among nearby nodes.** Devices communicate with each other to analyze data collectively.
- **Lower latency.** Since data doesn't travel over long distances, decisions can be made faster.
- **Reduced network bandwidth usage.** Only essential or summarized data may be sent to the cloud when needed.
- **Useful in applications with infrequent data collection.** For example, agricultural sensors that gather hourly measurements.
- **Often implemented using mesh networks.** Mesh communication lets nodes connect to each other directly, forming a cooperative network.

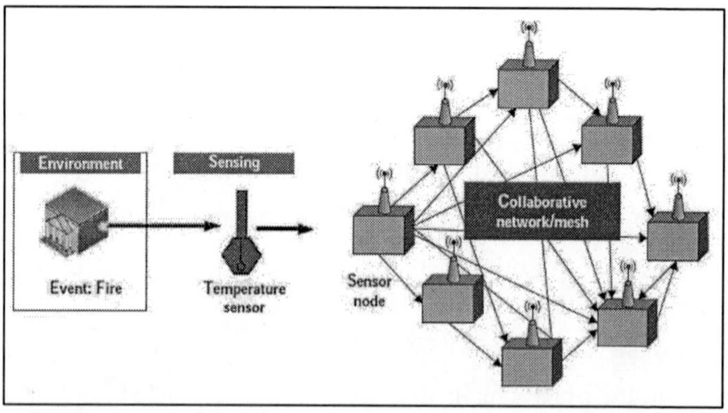

Fig. 2.4 Event detection using a collaborative processing topology

Explanation:

- Each **sensor node** can detect environmental parameters such as temperature, fire, or smoke.
- Nodes communicate directly with neighboring nodes, forming a **mesh network**.
- Data is **processed collaboratively**, reducing the need to send all raw data to a central server.
- This topology is **efficient for wide-area deployments**, lowers latency, and conserves network bandwidth.

Table 2.5

Processing Type	Location of Processing	Key Features	Example Application
On-Site Processing	Local (at the sensor node)	Real-time decision-making, low latency	Fire detection system
Remote Off-Site Processing	Cloud or server-based	Centralized analysis, requires internet connectivity	Smart home cloud services
Collaborative Processing	Distributed (among local nodes)	Shared resources, reduced bandwidth use	Agricultural monitoring

2.4 IoT Device Design and Selection Considerations

When designing an IoT system, the choice of **processor** is the most critical factor, as it governs the overall performance, usability, and cost of the device. Alongside the processor, several other factors play a significant role in the design and selection of IoT devices.

Key Considerations

- **Size:** The physical dimensions of a device influence both its **form factor** and energy consumption. Smaller devices are preferred for applications like wearables, where large form factors are impractical and consume more power.
- **Energy Consumption:** The energy needs of the processor and sensors determine battery life. Devices with higher energy demands require frequent battery replacements, reducing long-term sustainability, particularly in remote or unattended IoT deployments.
- **Cost:** The price of the processor and associated sensors directly affects deployment density. Lower-cost hardware allows for widespread deployment of multiple sensor nodes, enabling broader coverage for applications such as environmental or safety monitoring.
- **Memory:** Both **volatile and non-volatile memory** impact the device's ability to process, store, filter, and format data locally. Higher memory increases functionality but also raises the cost of the device.
- **Processing Power:** Processing capability determines the type of applications the IoT node can support. Devices handling complex tasks like video or image analysis require higher processing power compared to simple environmental sensing.
- **I/O Rating:** Input–output specifications of the processor define compatibility with sensors and peripherals. Modern processors often operate at **3.3 V**, while older devices used **5 V**, which may require additional voltage conversion circuitry, adding complexity and cost.
- **Add-ons and Integrated Features:** Features like **ADC units, built-in clocks, USB/ethernet interfaces, and wireless connectivity** enhance device functionality and reduce development time. Pre-integrated options simplify hardware integration and make development faster and more efficient.

2.5 Processing Offloading in IoT

Efficient processing distribution is essential for **energy-efficient, miniaturized, and scalable IoT systems**. IoT deployments typically include multiple layers of processing, ranging from local sensors to cloud-based systems.

Layers of IoT Data Processing

1. **Local Processing**
   - Immediate processing at the sensor node.
   - Follows an **on-site topology**.
   - Sensor nodes can be connected via wired or short-range wireless links.
   - Data can be processed locally or forwarded to higher layers.
2. **Edge Processing**
   - Utilizes devices within the local network to handle data.
   - Communication is usually via short-range wireless connections.
   - Data that requires cloud analysis is forwarded via long-range networks.
3. **Fog Processing**
   - Fog nodes operate over localized geographic areas, smaller than cloud coverage.
   - Often act as gateways for IoT devices to connect to the Internet.
   - Provides intermediate processing, storage, and network optimization.
4. **Cloud Processing**
   - Devices connect via long-range networks to cloud servers.
   - Enables large-scale data storage, advanced analytics, and AI applications.
   - Cloud processing may be **costly**, and latency, bandwidth, and system complexity are important considerations.

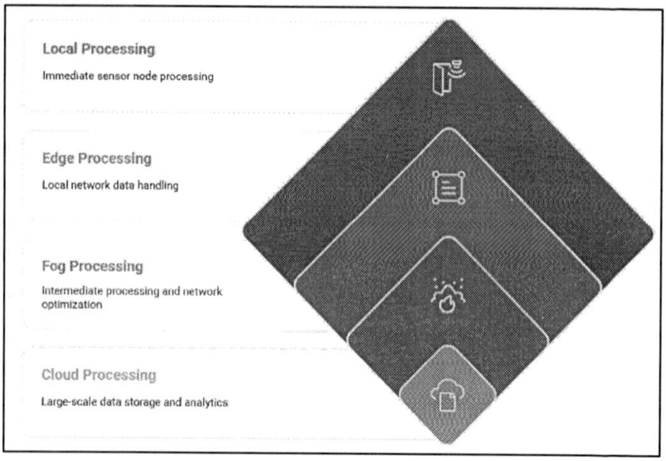

Fig. 2.5 Layers of IoT Data Processing

Data Offloading in IoT

Data offloading refers to the process of transferring computation and data from IoT devices to other processing layers to improve efficiency, reduce energy consumption, and optimize network usage. It can be broadly divided into three aspects:

Offload Location

Offload Decision Making

Offloading Considerations

Offload Location

The location where data is offloaded has a significant impact on cost, efficiency, and applicability of the IoT system. The main offload locations are:

1. Edge Offloading

- Data processing occurs close to the source, typically at or near the sensor node.
- Helps in **aggregating data**, reducing bandwidth usage, and performing local computations.

- Minimizes the load on the network and enables **low-latency responses**.

2. Fog Offloading

- Acts as an intermediate layer between the edge and the cloud.
- Helps **conserve bandwidth** while providing faster processing than cloud-only solutions.
- Ideal for applications requiring **quick mobility** or reduced dependence on the Internet.

3. Remote Server Offloading

- Data is sent to an external server with strong processing capabilities.
- Suitable for IoT devices with **limited local processing power**.
- Challenges include **scalability** and higher **maintenance costs**.

4. Cloud Offloading

- Data is transferred to cloud infrastructure for processing and storage.
- Provides **massive scalability**, on-demand resource allocation, and global accessibility.
- Ideal for **large-scale data analytics** and applications requiring high computational power.

Offload Decision Making

Offload decision-making determines **where, when, and how much data** should be transferred from IoT devices to other layers. This depends on:

- **Data generation rate** of devices
- **Available network bandwidth**
- **Criticality of the application**
- **Processing resources available**

There are three main approaches to offload decision-making:

(a) Naïve Approach

- Offloads data to the nearest available processing node based on simple rules.
- Easy to implement but not effective for **dense deployments** or **complex data types** like video and audio.

(b) Bargaining-Based Approach

- Uses optimization techniques to decide offloading, considering network congestion and QoS (Quality of Service).
- Focuses on optimizing critical performance parameters while compromising on less critical ones. .
- Example: **Game theory-based optimization** for network and computational resources.

(c) Learning-Based Approach

- Utilizes **historical data and patterns** of data flow to optimize offloading dynamically.
- Employs **machine learning** algorithms to improve overall system performance over time.
- Requires higher **processing power and memory** but enhances efficiency and predictive capabilities.

Offloading Considerations

Selecting an appropriate data offloading strategy requires careful evaluation of several key factors:

1. **Bandwidth**
   - Refers to the maximum amount of data that can be transmitted between two points in a network.
   - Higher bandwidth ensures efficient and faster data transfer over both wired and wireless connections.
2. **Latency**
   - The time delay between the initiation of data transfer and its completion.
   - Can be affected by network congestion or processing delays.
   - **Low latency** is essential for real-time IoT applications, such as autonomous vehicles or industrial automation.
3. **Criticality**
   - Measures the urgency or importance of the IoT application.
   - **Examples:**

- Fire detection systems → High criticality; require immediate response (milliseconds).
- Agricultural monitoring → Low criticality; can tolerate delayed responses (hours or days).

4. **Resources**

- Refers to the processing power, memory, and computational capabilities available at the offload location.
- **Examples:**
  - Real-time multimedia or video analytics → Requires high computational power and advanced analytics.
  - Simple scalar data processing (e.g., temperature, humidity) → Can be handled with minimal resources.

Exercise

MCQs (Multiple Choice Questions)

1. Which of the following is a common data format used in IoT?

a) XML

b) JSON

c) CSV

d) All of the above

Answer: d) All of the above

2. Edge computing in IoT primarily refers to:

a) Sending all data to the cloud

b) Processing data close to the data source

c) Using blockchain for IoT

d) None of the above

Answer: b) Processing data close to the data source

3. Which processing topology involves all IoT devices sending data directly to a central server?

a) Centralized

b) Decentralized

c) Distributed

d) Hierarchical

Answer: a) Centralized

4. Which factor is **not** considered while selecting IoT devices?

a) Energy consumption

b) Device color

c) Processing capability

d) Cost

Answer: b) Device color

5. Offloading processing from IoT devices to the cloud is mainly done to:

a) Increase latency

b) Reduce local processing load

c) Store more data locally

d) Increase device weight

Answer: b) Reduce local processing load

Very Short Answer Questions

1. Name two common data formats used in IoT.

2. What is edge processing in IoT?

3. Give one example of a centralized IoT processing system.

4. Mention one factor to consider while designing an IoT device.

5. Define processing offloading in IoT in one sentence.

Short Answer Questions

1. Differentiate between centralized and distributed processing topologies in IoT.

2. Why is the choice of data format important in IoT systems?

3. List the key factors to consider when designing and selecting IoT devices.

4. Explain the concept of processing offloading in IoT.

5. What is the significance of processing data in IoT for real-time applications?

Long Answer Questions

1. Explain the importance of processing in IoT and describe the different processing topologies.

2. Discuss the considerations for IoT device design and selection in detail.

3. Describe the concept of processing offloading in IoT, including its advantages and potential challenges.

4. Compare and contrast centralized, decentralized, and distributed IoT processing topologies with suitable examples.

5. How does edge computing improve the efficiency of IoT systems? Explain with scenarios.

Unit-3

Associated IOT Technologies

3.1 Cloud Computing- Introduction

Cloud computing has revolutionized the way individuals and organizations store, access, and manage data. It enables users to utilize applications and data over the Internet, eliminating the limitations of local storage or private servers. To understand its significance, it is helpful to compare traditional computing with the cloud-based approach.

Challenges Solved by Cloud Computing: Traditional vs. Cloud Approach

1. Traditional (On-Premises) Approach:

- Companies needed to purchase physical servers, storage devices, and networking hardware.
- This required significant upfront investment, known as **Capital Expenditure (CapEx)**.
- Businesses often had to estimate peak usage, frequently leading to over-provisioning and wasted resources.
- Deploying new servers or upgrading infrastructure could take **weeks or months**.

2. Cloud Computing Approach:

- Instead of owning hardware, businesses rent computing power from cloud providers such as AWS, Google Cloud, or Microsoft Azure.
- Costs shift from large upfront expenses to manageable **Operational Expenditure (OpEx)** in the form of monthly payments.
- Cloud computing eliminates delays, reduces resource wastage, and allows **on-demand scalability**.

Definition of Cloud Computing

Cloud computing is a technology that allows data and applications to be stored, accessed, and managed over the Internet rather than relying on local computers or private servers. This enables greater flexibility, scalability, and cost efficiency.

Cloud Computing Architecture

The architecture of cloud computing consists of several components that work together to provide seamless service delivery:

1. **Front-End Components:**
   - Interfaces used by the end-users to interact with cloud services.
   - Examples include **fat clients** (feature-rich applications) and **thin clients** (web-based interfaces).
2. **Back-End Components:**
   - Infrastructure that supports cloud services, including **servers, storage systems, and databases**.
3. **Cloud-Based Delivery and Network:**
   - The network infrastructure connecting users to cloud services.
   - Includes the **Internet, intranets, and inter-cloud networks** for data transfer and service delivery.

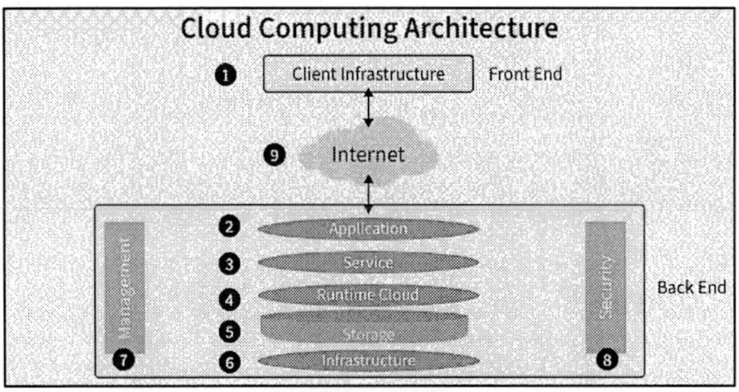

Fig. 3.1 Cloud Computing Architecture

1. Front-End (User Interaction)

The front-end of cloud computing focuses on the user interface, which is divided into two types of clients:

- **Thin Clients:** These rely on web browsers to provide lightweight and portable access to cloud services. They are ideal for users who need simple interaction without heavy software installation.

- **Fat Clients:** These offer rich functionality and a more robust user experience, often handling more processing locally while interacting with the cloud.

2. Back-End Platforms (Cloud Computing Engine)

The back-end forms the core of cloud computing, consisting of multiple servers and storage systems.

- **Servers:** Handle the application logic, process computations, and manage requests.
- **Storage Systems:** Ensure effective data handling and persistence.
- The combination of these components provides the necessary **processing power, storage capacity, and data management capabilities** that operate behind the scenes.

3. Cloud-Based Delivery and Network

Cloud computing delivers resources over networks such as the **Internet, Intranet, and Intercloud**:

- **Internet:** Enables global access to cloud services.
- **Intranet:** Supports internal communication within an organization.
- **Intercloud:** Facilitates interoperability between different cloud service providers.

This network setup ensures seamless access, data transfer, and connectivity for cloud applications.

Five Key Characteristics of Cloud Computing

1. On-Demand Self-Service: Users can automatically provision computing resources like storage and servers without manual intervention from the provider.

2. Broad Network Access: Cloud resources are available over networks and can be accessed through standard devices such as laptops, tablets, and smartphones.

3. **Resource Pooling:** Cloud providers pool resources to serve multiple clients using a multi-tenant model. Resources are dynamically allocated based on demand.

4. **Rapid Elasticity (Scalability):** Resources can be scaled up or down quickly, ensuring sufficient capacity during high-demand periods while avoiding waste during low usage.

5. **Measured Service (Pay-as-You-Go):** Cloud usage is monitored, controlled, and reported. Users pay only for the resources they actually consume, promoting cost efficiency.

Shared Responsibility Model

Security in the cloud is a joint responsibility between the provider and the customer:

- **Cloud Provider Responsibilities:** Includes securing the infrastructure, physical data centers, hardware, and core networking components.
- **Customer Responsibilities:** Involves securing data, managing access permissions, configuring firewalls, and protecting applications.

The exact division of responsibilities depends on the **service model** chosen, such as IaaS, PaaS, or SaaS.

3.2 Types of Cloud Computing Services

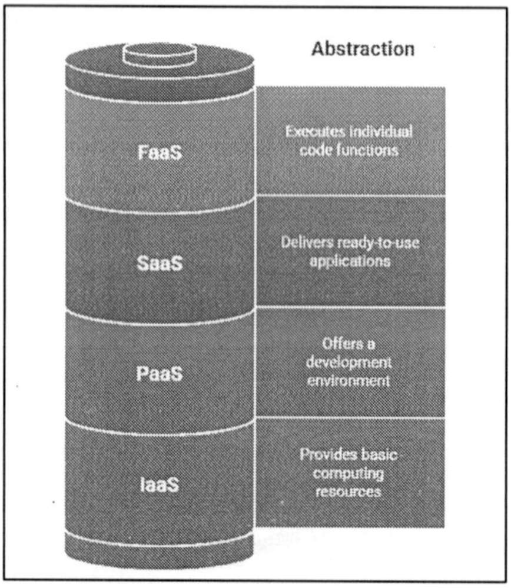

Fig. 3.2 Types of Cloud Computing

Cloud computing can be categorized into four main models:

1. **Infrastructure as a Service (IaaS)**
2. **Platform as a Service (PaaS)**
3. **Software as a Service (SaaS)**
4. **Function as a Service (FaaS)**

1. Infrastructure as a Service (IaaS)

IaaS is a cloud computing model that provides users with virtualized computing resources over the internet, including virtual machines, storage, and networking. Users do not need to manage physical hardware and only pay for the resources they consume.

Key Benefits of IaaS:

- **Flexibility and Control:** Users can access virtualized resources such as VMs, storage, and networks, giving them control over the operating system and applications.
- **Cost Reduction:** Eliminates the need for purchasing and

maintaining physical infrastructure, lowering capital expenditure.

- **Scalability:** Resources can be scaled up or down based on demand, ensuring performance optimization and cost efficiency.

2. Platform as a Service (PaaS)

PaaS is a cloud model where a provider delivers both hardware and software tools for developing, testing, and running applications. Users can focus on building applications while the provider manages the underlying infrastructure.

Example: AWS Elastic Beanstalk helps developers deploy and manage applications without worrying about servers, load balancing, or scaling.

Key Benefits of PaaS:

- **Simplified Development:** Developers can focus on coding and application logic while the platform handles infrastructure management.
- **Improved Efficiency:** Reduces the complexity of infrastructure management, accelerates development cycles, and streamlines updates.
- **Automated Scaling:** PaaS automatically manages resource scaling to ensure efficient workload handling.

3. Software as a Service (SaaS)

SaaS allows users to access software applications over the internet without installing them locally. The provider hosts and manages the software, including updates, maintenance, and storage.

Example: Google Docs enables users to create and share documents online without downloading any software.

Key Benefits of SaaS:

- **Accessibility and Collaboration:** Applications can be accessed from anywhere via the internet, promoting easy collaboration.
- **Automatic Updates:** Providers manage maintenance and updates, ensuring users always have the latest features and security enhancements.
- **Cost-Effectiveness:** Reduces the need for IT support and individual software licenses, lowering overall costs.

4. Function as a Service (FaaS)

Function as a Service (FaaS) is a cloud computing model that enables users to execute code in response to specific events without the need to manage the underlying servers or infrastructure. Developers simply write the code, deploy it to the cloud, and the provider runs it automatically when triggered. Billing is based only on the actual execution time of the code.

Example: Using **AWS Lambda**, a function can be set up to automatically resize images whenever a user uploads a photo to a website. There is no need to maintain a continuously running server, as the function executes only when the event occurs.

Key Advantages of FaaS:

- **Event-Driven Execution:** Functions are triggered automatically by specific events, reducing the need for server management.
- **Cost Efficiency:** Users are charged only for the time the function runs, making it a cost-effective solution.
- **Scalability and Agility:** Serverless architecture can automatically scale to handle varying workloads, allowing rapid deployment and flexible development.

Cloud Deployment Models

1. Private Cloud

- A dedicated cloud environment for a single organization.
- Can be managed internally or by a third-party provider.
- Offers maximum security and control.
- Can be hosted on-premises or off-premises.

2. Public Cloud

- Operated by third-party providers such as AWS or Google Cloud.
- Available to the general public via the internet.
- Provides scalable resources with a pay-as-you-go model.

3. **Hybrid Cloud**

- Combines private and public cloud environments.
- Allows data and applications to be shared between the two.
- Offers flexibility to maintain sensitive data privately while using public cloud resources for scalable workloads.

4. **Multi-Cloud**

- Involves using services from two or more different public cloud providers.
- Helps prevent vendor lock-in.
- Allows organizations to select the best services from each provider for specific needs.

Top Cloud Computing Providers

Several companies lead the cloud computing market, offering a variety of services and solutions to meet business and individual needs. Key details about these providers are summarized below:

Table 3.1

Company	Cloud Service Name	Key Offerings
1. Amazon	AWS (Amazon Web Services)	Compute, Storage, AI/ML, Databases, Networking
2. Microsoft	Azure	Cloud computing, AI, Analytics, Hybrid Cloud
3. Google	Google Cloud Platform (GCP)	AI/ML, Big Data, Kubernetes, Cloud Storage
4. Alibaba	Alibaba Cloud	IaaS, AI, Big Data, Cloud Security, CDN
5. Oracle	Oracle Cloud	Enterprise Cloud, Databases, SaaS, PaaS
6. IBM	IBM Cloud	AI, Quantum Computing,

		Hybrid Cloud, Security
7. Salesforce	Salesforce Cloud	CRM, SaaS, AI, Analytics
8. Tencent	Tencent Cloud	AI, Gaming Cloud, IoT, Big Data

Cloud Security

Cloud security refers to the set of practices and strategies implemented to safeguard data, applications, and infrastructure within cloud computing environments. Key measures include:

1. **Data Encryption**: Protecting data through encryption ensures that even if unauthorized parties intercept it, the information remains unreadable.
2. **Access Control**: Restricting access to sensitive data and resources using strict authentication methods ensures only authorized users can interact with cloud services.
3. **Multi-Factor Authentication (MFA)**: MFA strengthens security by requiring users to verify their identity through multiple methods, such as passwords, biometrics, or security tokens, before accessing cloud applications.

Common Use Cases of Cloud Computing

Cloud computing is widely applied across various sectors for multiple purposes:

- **Scalable Websites and Applications:** Host platforms that can handle millions of simultaneous users.
- **Data Storage, Backup, and Recovery:** Efficiently store large amounts of data and recover it quickly in case of system failures.
- **Big Data Analytics:** Analyze large datasets and extract actionable insights.
- **Software Development and Testing:** Rapidly set up and dismantle development environments to streamline the software lifecycle.

- **Artificial Intelligence and Machine Learning:** Leverage high-performance computing resources for training AI and ML models.

3.3 Virtualization

Virtualization allows a single physical computer to operate as multiple independent virtual machines. Traditionally, computers performed only one task at a time, often leaving much of their capacity unused. Virtualization optimizes hardware usage by enabling multiple virtual systems to run simultaneously on a single physical machine.

In cloud computing, providers use virtualization to partition a single server into multiple virtual servers. This approach allows businesses to utilize only the resources they need, reducing the cost and avoiding the need for additional hardware.

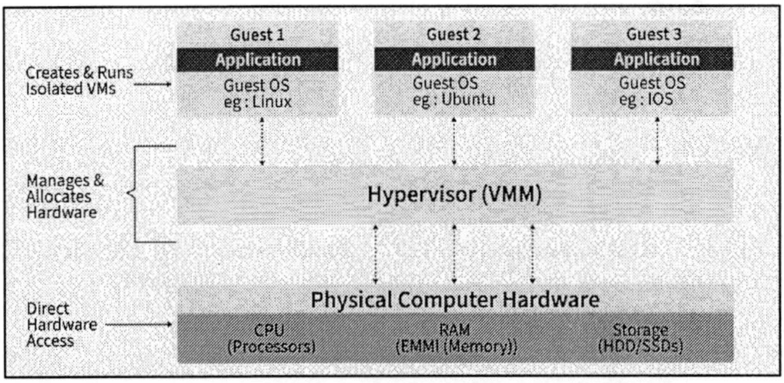

Fig. 3.3 Type 1 Virtualization (Bare-Metal)

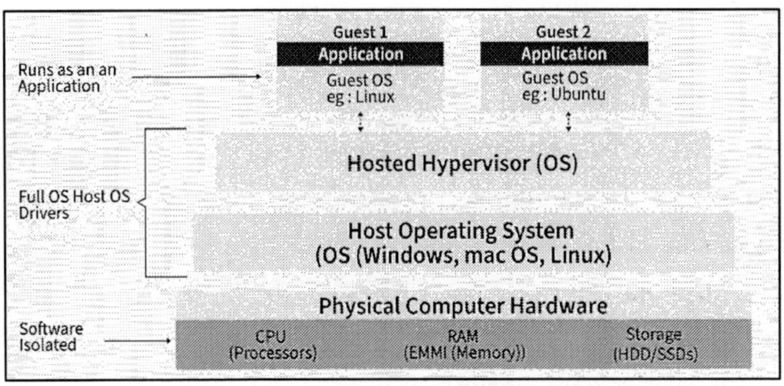

Fig. 3.4 Type 2 Virtualization (Hosted)

Understanding Virtualization with a Real-World Example

Consider a company that needs servers for four different purposes:

1. Storing customer data securely
2. Hosting an online shopping website
3. Processing employee payroll
4. Running social media marketing software

Each of these tasks has specific requirements:

- The customer data server needs ample storage and a Windows OS.
- The online shopping platform requires a high-traffic server with a Linux OS.
- The payroll system demands more RAM and a particular OS version.

Initially, the company would have to purchase four separate physical servers, maintain them, and upgrade them individually, which can be costly.

By implementing **virtualization**, the company can run these applications on fewer physical servers using multiple **virtual machines (VMs)**. Each VM functions as an independent server with its own OS and resources. This approach reduces costs, optimizes resource use, and allows centralized management.

How Virtualization Works

Virtualization relies on software called a **hypervisor** to create multiple virtual computers on a single physical machine. These virtual machines operate like separate computers but share the host's physical resources.

Virtual Machines (VMs)

- VMs can be created after installing virtualization software.
- They function like standard applications but operate as independent computers.
- The physical computer is called the **host**, and the virtual machines are called **guests**.
- One host can support multiple guest VMs.
- Each guest VM can run its own OS, which may be different from

the host OS.

- VMs act like standalone computers with their own configurations, programs, and settings.
- They share CPU, RAM, and storage resources but operate as if they have their own dedicated hardware.

Hypervisors

A **hypervisor** is software that enables virtualization by managing how virtual machines use the host's resources. It acts as an intermediary between the physical hardware and the VMs.

For example, if a VM needs extra computing power, the hypervisor allocates the required resources from the host hardware.

Types of Hypervisors:

1. **Type 1 (Bare-Metal Hypervisor):**
   - Installed directly on the physical hardware, without an underlying OS.
   - Offers high efficiency due to direct access to system resources.
2. **Type 2 Hypervisor:**
   - Runs on top of an existing OS like Windows or macOS.
   - Suitable when multiple OS environments need to run on the same machine.

3.4 Types of Virtualization

1. **Application Virtualization:** Runs applications in isolated environments without installing them on the host OS.
2. **Network Virtualization:** Combines hardware and software network resources into a single virtual network.
3. **Desktop Virtualization:** Allows desktop environments to be hosted on a central server and accessed remotely.
4. **Storage Virtualization:** Pools multiple storage devices to appear as a single storage resource.
5. **Server Virtualization:** Runs multiple virtual servers on a single

physical server to optimize resource usage.

6. **Data Virtualization:** Provides a unified view of data from different sources without moving it physically.

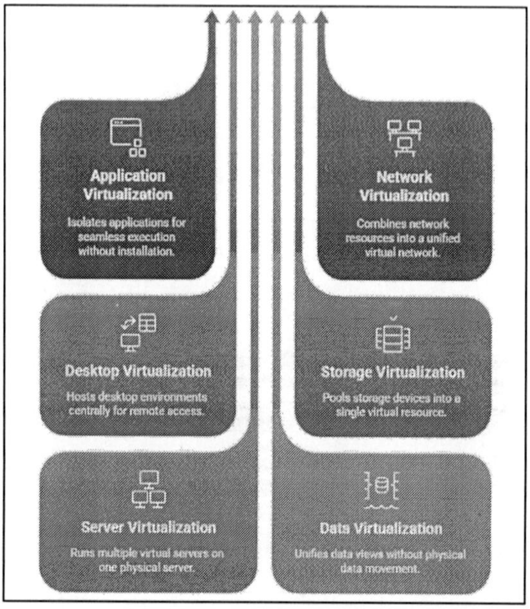

Fig. 3.5 Types of Virtualization

1. **Application Virtualization**: Application virtualization allows users to run software directly from a remote server without installing it on their local devices. The application's settings and personal data are stored on the server, but users can interact with it as if it were installed locally. This approach is particularly useful when different versions of the same software need to be accessed by multiple users.

Example: Microsoft Azure enables employees to access applications through the cloud without installing them on their own computers. Once the application is set up on Azure, users can access it from any device such as laptops or tablets. Although it feels like the software is running locally, the actual processing happens on Azure's servers. This approach improves speed, security, and convenience for organizations.

2. Network Virtualization: Network virtualization allows multiple virtual networks to operate on a single physical network, each functioning independently. It enables the creation of virtual routers, switches, firewalls, and VPNs, providing more flexibility and simplifying network management.

Example: Google Cloud provides tools for network virtualization, allowing companies to set up their own virtual networks using software rather than physical devices. Tasks such as assigning IP addresses, configuring firewalls, and establishing private connections can all be done in the cloud. This method reduces hardware costs, saves time, and provides the ability to scale and modify networks easily.

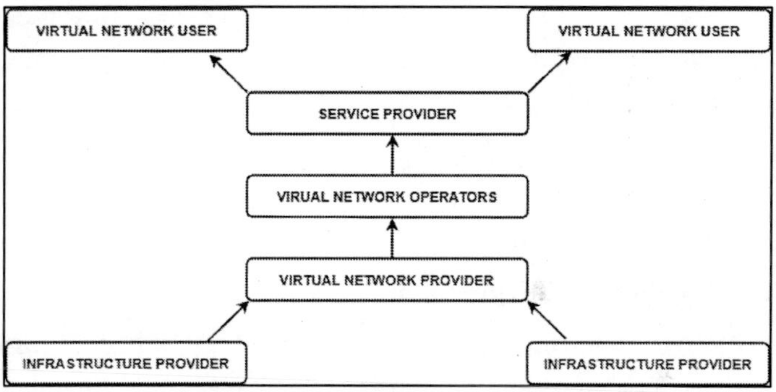

Fig. 3.6 Network Virtualization

3. Desktop Virtualization

Desktop virtualization allows multiple virtual desktops to be created, which users can access from any device such as laptops, tablets, or smartphones. This setup offers flexibility, simplifies software updates, and ensures that users can work from anywhere without needing dedicated physical machines.

Example: An educational technology company like GeeksforGeeks uses services such as Amazon Work Spaces or Google Cloud Virtual Desktops to provide its team members with a consistent coding environment. Employees can log in from any device and access a fully functional virtual desktop in the cloud. This approach simplifies management, improves security, and reduces the need for individual physical computers for every user.

4. Storage Virtualization

Storage virtualization merges storage resources from multiple servers into a single, manageable system. This improves performance, simplifies administration, and ensures that operations continue smoothly even if the underlying hardware changes or fails.

Example: Amazon S3 is a common example of storage virtualization. Large companies can store vast amounts of data in a centralized, cloud-based location. Employees and systems can access this data securely from anywhere, without worrying about hardware limitations or local storage issues.

5. Server Virtualization

Server virtualization divides a single physical server into multiple virtual servers, each running independently. This enhances resource utilization, reduces costs, and simplifies server management, migration, and energy consumption.

Example: A startup with a single high-performance server can use virtualization platforms like VMware vSphere, Microsoft Hyper-V, or KVM to create multiple virtual machines (VMs). Each VM operates as a separate server, with its own operating system (Windows or Linux) and dedicated applications. For instance, one VM can host a web server, another a database server, and a third a file server. This setup lowers operational costs, facilitates easier backups and recovery, and allows quick restoration if one VM encounters issues.

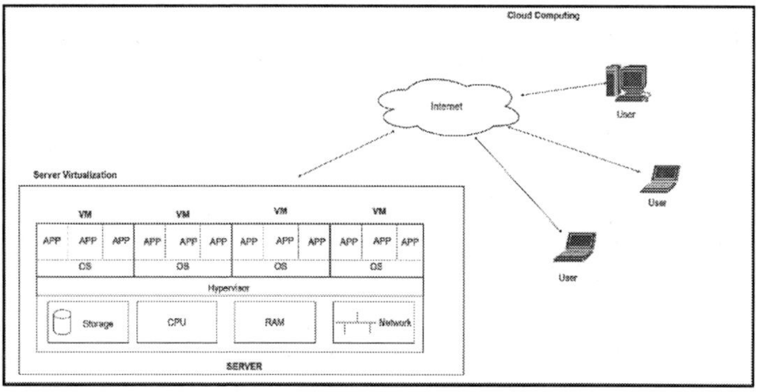

Fig. 3.7 Server Virtualization

6. Data Virtualization

Data virtualization integrates information from multiple sources into a single, cohesive view without requiring knowledge of where or how the data is physically stored. This allows users to access and interact with data remotely through cloud-based services.

Example: Companies like Oracle and IBM provide data virtualization platforms that enable organizations to unify their data for analytics, reporting, and operational decision-making without moving the original data.

Key Benefits of Virtualization in Cloud Computing

- **Cost Efficiency:** Reduces the need for multiple physical servers, lowering hardware costs, maintenance, and energy consumption.
- **Enhanced Resource Utilization:** Maximizes the use of available computing power, storage, and network resources that might otherwise remain underused.
- **Scalability and Flexibility:** Enables rapid scaling of resources to match changing workloads without downtime or additional hardware purchases.
- **Improved Disaster Recovery:** Simplifies backup and recovery processes, allowing virtual machines to be quickly restored or replicated

even if physical servers fail.

- **Stronger Security:** Virtual machines (VMs) are isolated from one another, so a compromise in one VM doesn't impact others on the same host.
- **Agility and Flexibility:** Supports multiple operating systems on a single server and simplifies migration or management across different hardware environments.
- **Support for Legacy Systems:** Allows older applications to run in virtual environments, extending their usability and avoiding costly migrations.

Advantages for End Users

- **Flexibility and Accessibility:** Users can access applications and data from any device, anywhere, since everything is hosted in a virtual environment. Multiple operating systems can also be used on a single physical machine.
- **Reliability and Availability:** Virtualization enhances uptime. If a physical server fails, VMs can be quickly restored or moved to other servers, minimizing disruption. VMs are also isolated, so one failure doesn't affect others.
- **Enhanced Security:** VM isolation improves security, and virtual environments allow safe testing of applications and patches in a controlled "sandbox" before deployment.
- **Rapid Deployment and Easier Management:** New VMs can be provisioned in minutes, enabling faster access to applications. Entire virtual machines can also be migrated between servers without complicated reinstallation processes.

Advantages for Cloud Service Providers (CSPs)

1. **Optimized Resource Utilization:**

- Cloud resources are dynamically allocated to users based on their current needs.

- A resource assigned to one user at a particular time can later be reassigned to another user, enabling efficient reuse and maximizing resource efficiency.

2. Revenue Generation Opportunities:

- Cloud providers earn revenue from users based on the resources they consume.
- For example, if User A utilizes a storage service for a limited period, the provider earns revenue during that usage. Once User A releases the storage, the same resources can be allocated to User B, generating additional income.
- This approach allows cloud providers to continuously monetize their infrastructure and improve profitability.

3.5 Service Level Agreements (SLAs)

A **Service Level Agreement (SLA)** is a formal commitment between a cloud service provider and a client that defines the expected performance and quality of service. SLAs act as a contract or agreement that ensures both parties understand their responsibilities and expectations.

Types of SLAs

SLAs can be categorized into the following types:

1. **Customer-Based SLA:** Tailored for an individual customer and covers all services used by that customer.
2. **Service-Based SLA:** Standardized SLA for a specific service offered to all clients.
3. **Multilevel SLA:** Combines different levels of SLAs to meet the needs of various customers and organizational units.

Some SLAs are legally enforceable, while others function more like **Operational Level Agreements (OLAs)**. Consulting a legal professional before finalizing major SLAs is recommended.

Key Parameters Specified in SLAs

SLAs typically define metrics such as:

- **Service Availability (Uptime):** The guaranteed operational time of the service.
- **Latency / Response Time:** Maximum acceptable delay in service responses.
- **Reliability of Service Components:** The stability and proper functioning of service elements.
- **Accountability:** Responsibilities of both the service provider and the client.
- **Warranties:** Guarantees and commitments related to service performance.

If a cloud provider fails to meet the agreed targets, they may be required to pay penalties to the client, similar to an insurance arrangement.

Examples of Cloud SLAs

1. **Windows Azure SLA:**
   - Guarantees 99.95% external connectivity for clients deploying two or more role instances across separate fault and upgrade domains.
   - Monitors all role instances and guarantees 99.9% detection when a role instance fails to start or operate correctly.
2. **SQL Azure SLA:**
   - Ensures database connectivity with an availability of 99.9% per month.
   - Availability is measured as the ratio of actual uptime to total time in a 30-day month.
   - Any denied connections due to the service are counted as downtime, and availability calculations are made for the full month.

SLAs and Usage Models

SLAs often depend on the usage model:

- **Pay-as-you-go resources:** Premium pricing may apply, and standard SLAs are provided to guarantee service performance.
- **Subscription-based resources:** Clients may subscribe to specific levels of service to ensure access to guaranteed resources, especially under

peak load conditions.

By clearly defining expectations, responsibilities, and penalties, SLAs protect both the client and the provider, ensuring reliable and accountable cloud service delivery.

SLA Lifecycle

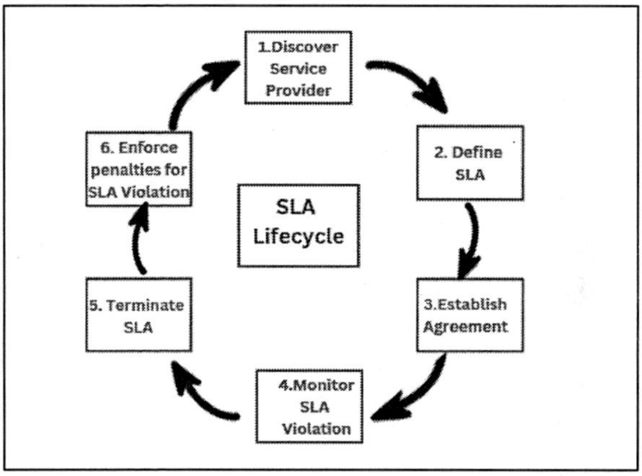

Fig. 3.8 SLA Lifecycle

SLA Lifecycle Steps

1. Identify Service Provider: The first step is to find a cloud or service provider capable of delivering the required services. This can involve researching providers, requesting proposals, or contacting vendors to evaluate their capabilities.

2. Define SLA Requirements: Once a provider is identified, both parties agree on the service level requirements. This includes defining **service level objectives (SLOs)**, metrics, and performance targets that will measure the provider's effectiveness.

3. Establish Agreement: After finalizing the requirements, a formal SLA is created. This document outlines the terms and conditions, including service expectations, reporting procedures, and penalties for non-compliance.

4. **Monitor SLA Compliance:** Continuous monitoring is essential to ensure the service provider meets agreed-upon targets. Any violations are tracked, reported, and addressed promptly.

5. **Terminate SLA if Needed:** If the service provider consistently fails to meet expectations, the SLA can be terminated either through mutual consent or by enforcing contractual penalties.

6. **Enforce Penalties for Violations:** When the provider breaches the SLA, penalties outlined in the agreement are applied. These may include financial fines, reduced service levels, or termination of the contract.

Advantages of SLAs

1. **Enhanced Communication:** SLAs provide a clear framework for communication, specifying the expected service levels. This ensures both the provider and client are aligned in their understanding of service expectations.

2. **Increased Accountability:** Providers are held responsible for delivering agreed-upon service quality. SLAs give clients a mechanism to hold providers accountable if performance falls short.

3. **Alignment with Business Objectives:** SLAs ensure that the services provided support the client's business goals by defining measurable performance targets and expectations.

4. **Minimized Downtime:** By setting protocols for issue resolution and monitoring, SLAs help reduce service interruptions and their impact on operations.

5. **Cost Efficiency:** Clear performance metrics and reporting allow clients to track service quality and manage costs effectively, ensuring value for money and avoiding unnecessary expenses.

Disadvantages of SLA

1. **Complexity:** SLAs can be complex to create and maintain and may require significant resources to implement and enforce.

2. **Rigidity:** SLAs can be rigid and may not be flexible enough to accommodate changing business needs or service requirements.

3. **Limited service options:** SLAs can limit the service options available to the customer, as the service provider may only be able to offer the specific services outlined in the agreement.

4. **Misaligned incentives:** SLAs may misalign incentives between the service provider and the customer, as the provider may focus on meeting the agreed-upon service levels rather than on providing the best service possible.

5. **Limited liability:** SLAs are not legal binding contracts and often limited the liability of the service provider in case of service failure.

3.6 Cloud Implementation

The requirement for cloud computing is rapidly increasing with the deployment of IOT Infrastructure for different applications. The Real deployment of the cloud is a Complex and costly procedure. There there is a requirement for simulating the system through a simulator before real implementation. A cloud simulator helps to model various kinds of cloud applications by creating data centers, virtual machines and other utilities that can be configured appropriately, thus making it easier to analyze. To date many cloud simulators had been developed and are being actively used to conduct cloud research. These simulators varies in features like availability of GUI, licensing, base programming language, extensibility etc. there are several research papers which already studied various cloud simulation tools. In this article I present a comprehensive study of major cloud simulators by highlighting their features and analyzing their pros and cons. A table containing comparative analysis of cloud simulators is available at the end of this article.

Benefits provided by simulators over establishing a physical cloud are as follows:

- **Minimal Cost:** Purchasing software costs less when compared to purchasing hardware and proprietary software (operating systems, hypervisor etc). Also many simulators are available free of cost.

- **Repeatable and Controllable:** We can test our experimental set up (simulation) as many times as we want until we get the desirable output.
- **Environment:** A simulator provides environment for evaluation of various scenarios under different workloads.

Cloud Simulators

Several simulation tools are available to model and test cloud computing environments, including **CloudSim, CloudAnalyst, and Green Cloud**. These simulators help researchers and developers evaluate cloud infrastructure, resource allocation policies, and application performance without the need for real cloud resources.

CloudSim

CloudSim is one of the most widely used simulation frameworks for cloud computing. It is an **event-driven simulator** built on top of **GridSim**, a grid computing simulation toolkit. CloudSim is written in **Java**, a popular object-oriented programming language, making it easy to extend and customize. Being **open-source**, it allows users to freely modify and enhance its functionality.

A unique feature of CloudSim is its **federated policy**, which enables simulation of cloud systems combining both private and public resources—a capability not commonly found in other simulators.

Key Features of CloudSim

- Supports modeling and simulation of **large-scale cloud computing environments**.
- Provides a comprehensive platform for **cloud infrastructure, service brokers, and resource provisioning policies**.
- Simulates **network connections** between various components of the cloud system.
- Facilitates the simulation of **federated cloud environments**, combining resources from multiple domains.
- Includes a **virtualization engine** to create and manage multiple

independent or co-hosted virtual services on a data center node.

- Offers flexibility in allocating processing cores to virtualized services using either **space-shared** or **time-shared** policies.

Architecture of CloudSim

CloudSim's architecture supports modular simulation of data centers, virtual machines, users, and network components, allowing detailed experimentation with cloud resource management and scheduling policies.

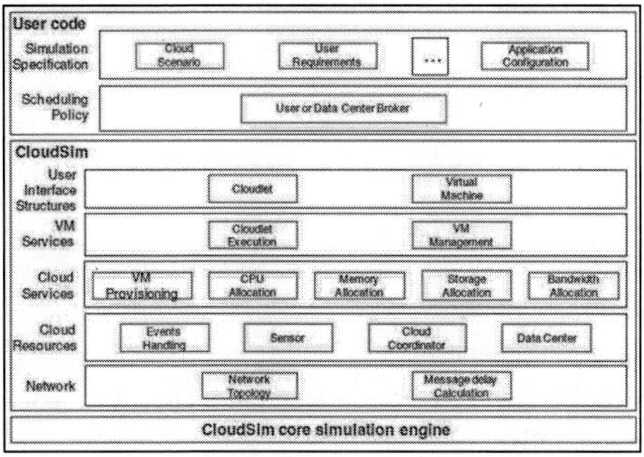

Fig. 3.9 Cloud Architecture

Despite many features of CloudSim, one major drawback is the lack of Graphical User Interface (GUI). According to R. Kanniga Devi et al. [6] CloudSim is the frequently used (nearly 23 experiments and may be more) simulation tool for cloud research.

CloudAnalyst

CloudAnalyst is a cloud simulation tool developed by Wickremasinghe as an extension of **CloudSim**. It was designed specifically to **analyze the performance of large-scale distributed cloud applications** that handle heavy workloads from users distributed across multiple geographic locations.

Key Features of CloudAnalyst

- **User-Friendly GUI**: Offers an intuitive graphical interface for easy simulation setup and analysis.
- **Highly Configurable Simulations**: Users can define simulations with extensive flexibility, adjusting parameters to match real-world scenarios.
- **Repeatable Experiments**: Simulations can be repeated with minor changes to observe the impact of adjustments.
- **Graphical Results**: Generates outputs in the form of **charts and tables** for clear visualization of results.
- **Extensible and Consolidated Technology**: Built for easy integration and extension, enabling users to customize functionality for specific needs.

Architecture of CloudAnalyst

CloudAnalyst's architecture builds on the CloudSim core but adds modules to handle **user bases, data centers, workload distribution, and visual representation**, allowing detailed analysis of cloud applications' response times, costs, and resource utilization.

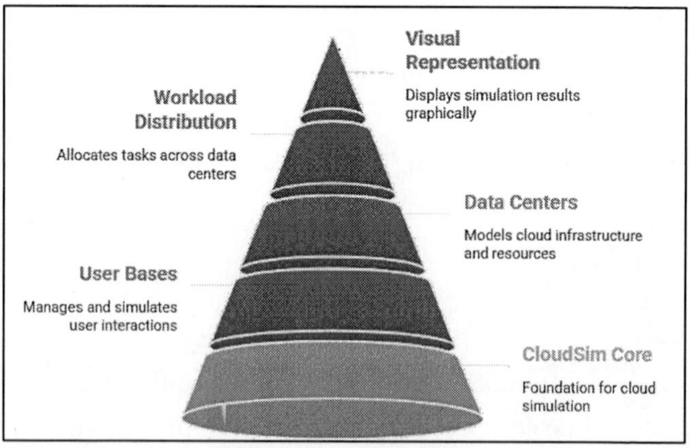

Fig. 3.10 CloudAnalyst Architecture

CloudAnalyst

CloudAnalyst provides a user-friendly graphical interface to simulate and configure **geographically distributed cloud systems**. Users can define various aspects of their cloud environment, including:

- The **geographic location of users** generating traffic
- The **location of data centers**
- The **number of users per data center**
- The **number of resources allocated to each data center**

CloudAnalyst can **generate outputs as charts or tables**, summarizing system performance and user statistics over the simulation period. By using this tool, cloud application developers can **identify optimal strategies for resource allocation**, choose the most suitable data center to handle specific requests, and **minimize associated costs**.

GreenCloud

GreenCloud is a **packet-level simulator** developed as an extension of the NS2 network simulator, with a strong focus on **energy-efficient cloud computing**. It is specifically designed to **measure energy consumption at different data center components**, such as switches, links, gateways, and packet-level communications, while also providing insights into workload distribution.

Key Features of GreenCloud

- Emphasis on **cloud networking and energy efficiency**
- Simulation of **CPU, memory, storage, and network resources**
- Independent **energy models** for each type of resource
- Support for **virtualization and VM migration**
- **Network-aware resource allocation**
- Complete **TCP/IP protocol implementation**
- User-friendly **GUI**
- **Open-source** platform

Architecture of GreenCloud

GreenCloud's architecture enables detailed simulation of **cloud infrastructure, energy consumption, and network traffic**, allowing researchers and developers to optimize energy usage and resource allocation in data centers.

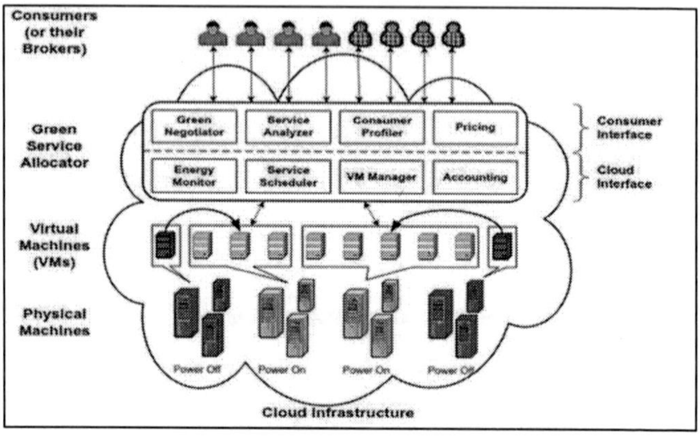

Fig. 3.11 GreenCloud Architecture

GreenCloud Drawbacks

While **GreenCloud** is a powerful simulator for energy-aware cloud environments, it has certain limitations:

- **High Simulation Time and Memory Usage:** Running simulations can take several minutes and require significant memory, which limits scalability to smaller data centers.
- **Steep Learning Curve:** Researchers need to be familiar with both **C++** and **OTcl libraries** to effectively use GreenCloud.
- **Specialized Use Case:** This simulator is primarily suited for studies focused on **energy consumption** in cloud data centers rather than general cloud simulation tasks.

OpenStack: An Open-Source Cloud Platform

OpenStack is a free, open-source cloud computing platform that emerged on **July 21, 2010** as a joint initiative by **NASA** and **Rackspace Hosting**. It provides **Infrastructure-as-a-Service (IaaS)** for both public and private clouds, enabling users to access virtual resources such as storage, compute, and networking without managing physical hardware. OpenStack abstracts resources via **APIs**, allowing administrators and users to directly interact with cloud services rather than managing the hardware manually.

OpenStack Components

OpenStack consists of several interconnected projects, with **nine key services** forming the core of the platform:

1. **Nova (Compute Service):** Manages computing resources including creating, deleting, and scheduling virtual machines. It automates resource allocation for virtualization and high-performance computing.
2. **Neutron (Networking Service):** Handles network connectivity within OpenStack. It manages networks and IP addresses using an API-driven approach.
3. **Swift (Object Storage):** Provides highly reliable object storage for unstructured data, accessible via RESTful APIs. It offers redundancy and can manage petabytes of data across clustered servers.
4. **Cinder (Block Storage):** Offers persistent block storage that users can provision and manage via APIs, allowing flexible control over storage requirements.
5. **Keystone (Identity Service):** Provides authentication and authorization services across OpenStack components, maintaining a central directory of users and services.
6. **Glance (Image Service):** Manages virtual disk images by registering, storing, and retrieving them from multiple backend systems.
7. **Horizon (Dashboard):** Offers a web-based interface to monitor, manage, and provision cloud resources easily.
8. **Ceilometer (Telemetry):** Tracks resource usage for billing and monitoring purposes and can trigger alarms when thresholds are exceeded.

9. **Heat (Orchestration):** Supports on-demand provisioning, auto-scaling, and orchestration of resources in coordination with telemetry services.

These core services manage **compute, storage, networking, identity, and orchestration**, forming the backbone of the OpenStack ecosystem.

Features of OpenStack

- **Modular Architecture:** Users can deploy only the components they require, making the platform customizable and scalable.
- **Multi-Tenancy Support:** Enables multiple users to securely share the same cloud infrastructure.
- **Open-Source:** OpenStack is free to use and modify, allowing organizations to tailor the platform to their needs without licensing costs.
- **Distributed Architecture:** Supports horizontal scaling across multiple physical servers, improving performance and workload handling.
- **API-Driven:** All services can be accessed and automated via APIs, facilitating integration with other tools.
- **Comprehensive Dashboard:** Provides a user-friendly interface for managing cloud resources, simplifying monitoring and administration.
- **Resource Pooling:** Allows dynamic allocation and de-allocation of compute, storage, and network resources, optimizing utilization and reducing waste.

Advantages of using OpenStack

- It boosts rapid provisioning of resources due to which orchestration and scaling up and down of resources becomes easy.
- Deployment of applications using OpenStack does not consume a large amount of time.
- Since resources are scalable therefore they are used more wisely and efficiently.
- The regulatory compliances associated with its usage are manageable.

Disadvantages of using OpenStack

- OpenStack is not very robust when orchestration is considered.
- Even today, the APIs provided and supported by OpenStack are not compatible with many of the hybrid cloud providers, thus integrating solutions becomes difficult.
- Like all cloud service providers OpenStack services also come with the risk of security breaches.

Amazon Web Services – A Commercial Cloud

Amazon Web Services (AWS) provides a comprehensive suite of **Internet of Things (IoT) products** designed to support a vast ecosystem of connected devices. AWS IoT products can be broadly classified into three categories:

1. **Device Software:** Includes tools and services that run directly on devices, such as **FreeRTOS** (a real-time operating system for microcontrollers) and **AWS IoT Greengrass** (enables local compute, messaging, and data caching on devices).
2. **Connectivity & Control Services:** Services in this category handle device connectivity, security, and management. Key services include **AWS IoT Core**, **AWS IoT Device Defender**, and **AWS IoT Device Management**.
3. **Analytics Services:** These services enable processing, analyzing, and visualizing IoT data. Notable offerings include **AWS IoT Events**, **AWS IoT Analytics**, **AWS IoT SiteWise**, and **AWS IoT ThingsGraph**.

What is AWS IoT?

AWS IoT is a cloud platform designed to manage **billions of connected devices**, ranging from consumer smart-home gadgets to industrial machinery. It allows organizations to **collect, process, and analyze data** from IoT devices in real time. The platform provides a **secure, scalable, and fully managed environment**, enabling businesses to focus on developing IoT solutions without worrying about infrastructure. Typical use cases include:

- Real-time monitoring of devices
- Remote device management
- Predictive maintenance
- Automation across various industries

Operational Framework of AWS IoT

AWS IoT enables devices to connect to the cloud and communicate with other devices, applications, or external services. Its workflow can be summarized as follows:

1. **Device Connectivity:** Devices connect to AWS using secure protocols like **MQTT**, **HTTP**, or **WebSockets**. Each device receives a unique identity for authentication and tracking.

2. **Data Collection and Processing:** Connected devices send data to **AWS IoT Core**, which acts as the central hub. Data can be filtered, transformed, and routed to other AWS services such as **AWS Lambda**, **Amazon Kinesis**, or **Amazon S3** for further processing.

3. **Analytics and Actions:** AWS IoT supports real-time analytics to generate insights. Businesses can define rules to trigger alerts, execute automated actions, or send commands back to devices, enabling **data-driven decision-making**.

4. **Device Management:** Using **AWS IoT Device Management**, organizations can organize, monitor, and remotely manage their fleet of devices. Features include firmware updates, device health tracking, and policy management for large-scale deployments.

5. **Security:** AWS IoT incorporates multiple layers of security, including **device authentication**, **identity and access management (IAM)**, and **data encryption**, ensuring safe communication and device integrity.

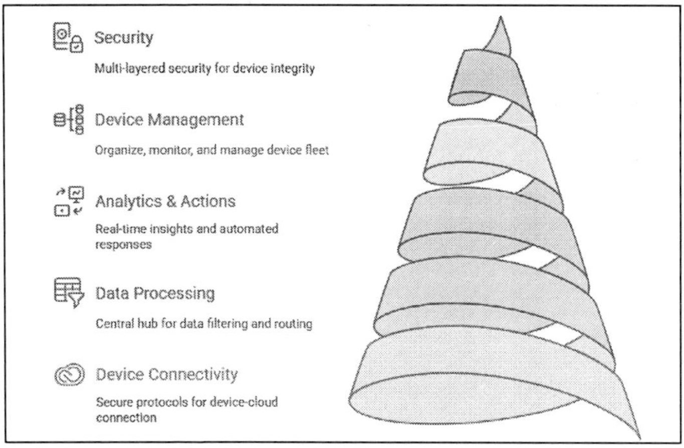

Fig. 3.12 AWS IOT WorkFlow

AWS IoT Services

Amazon Web Services (AWS) offers a comprehensive suite of IoT services, categorized into **Device Software**, **Connectivity & Control Services**, and **Analytics Services**. Each category is designed to address different aspects of managing IoT devices and data.

1. Device Software

AWS provides robust tools for edge devices, allowing applications to run locally while maintaining cloud connectivity. These tools help deploy, manage, and secure software directly at the edge.

- **AWS IoT Greengrass:** This service allows you to build, deploy, and manage applications on edge devices. Greengrass enables devices in homes, factories, and other business environments to run IoT applications locally while seamlessly connecting to the cloud.
- **AWS FreeRTOS:** FreeRTOS is an open-source real-time operating system for microcontrollers. It simplifies the deployment, security, and management of low-power devices, enabling efficient operation and reduced dependency on constant cloud connectivity.

2. Connectivity & Control Services

These services provide secure and reliable ways to connect, monitor, and manage devices from the cloud. They give organizations centralized control over their IoT ecosystem, ensuring devices are authenticated, secure, and easily manageable.

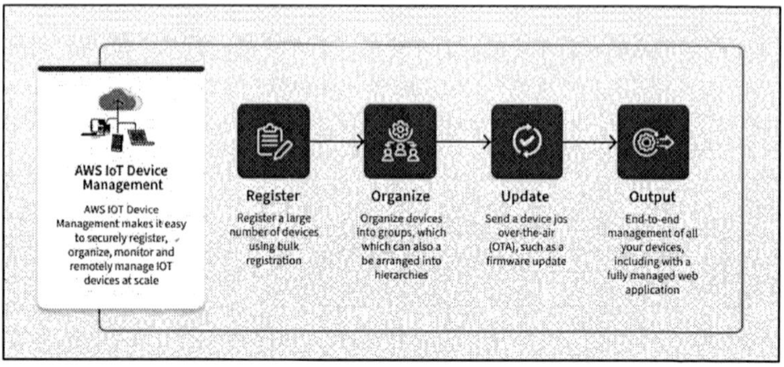

Fig. 3.13 AWS IOT Device Management

2. Connectivity & Control Services

AWS offers services that allow secure, reliable, and centralized management of IoT devices, ensuring smooth communication and robust security across your IoT ecosystem.

- **AWS IoT Core:** IoT Core enables devices to connect and communicate securely with cloud applications as well as with other devices. It provides a dependable framework for real-time interactions, ensuring data flows efficiently and reliably.
- **AWS IoT Device Defender:** This service continuously monitors IoT devices for potential security risks. It audits configurations, detects anomalies, and ensures devices adhere to recommended security best practices, helping maintain a secure IoT environment.
- **AWS IoT Device Management:** Device Management simplifies large-scale IoT operations by allowing secure device registration, organization, monitoring, and remote management. It helps organizations efficiently scale and maintain control over their entire fleet of connected devices.

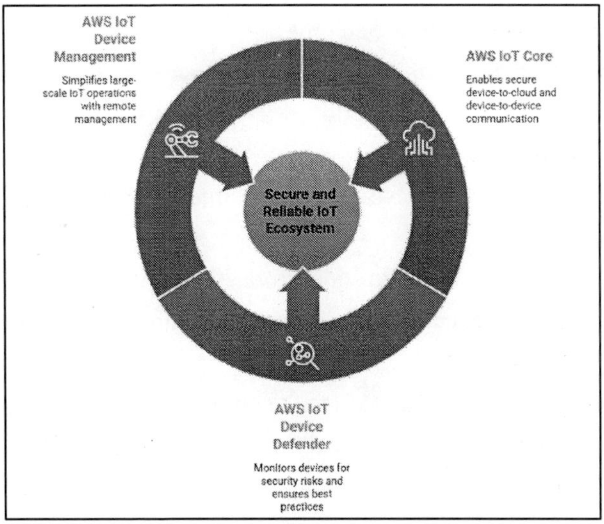

Fig. 3.14 Connectivity & Control Services

3. AWS IoT Analytics

AWS IoT Analytics is a comprehensive service that enables businesses to process, analyze, and gain insights from large volumes of IoT data. It streamlines data workflows, allowing organizations to make informed decisions efficiently.

- **AWS IoT SiteWise:** Designed for industrial environments, SiteWise simplifies the collection, structuring, and analysis of operational data, helping companies optimize performance at scale.
- **AWS IoT Events:** This service detects events in real time, identifying patterns and triggering automated actions based on changes detected from IoT sensors and applications, ensuring timely responses.
- **AWS IoT Things Graph:** A visual tool that connects IoT devices and cloud services, enabling the development of complex IoT applications with minimal coding while maintaining seamless interoperability.

Benefits of AWS IoT

Leveraging AWS IoT offers several advantages that improve efficiency, security, and overall business outcomes:

- **Scalability:** Supports billions of devices and trillions of messages, making it suitable for large-scale IoT deployments.
- **Cost Efficiency:** Operates on a pay-as-you-go model, reducing the need for heavy upfront infrastructure investments and allowing efficient resource allocation.
- **Enhanced Security:** Provides robust security features including encryption, identity management, and secure communication protocols to protect data and devices.
- **Real-Time Insights:** Offers analytics and machine learning capabilities to monitor devices in real time and generate predictive insights for faster, data-driven decision-making.
- **Automation and Operational Efficiency:** Enables automation of repetitive tasks, streamlining operations and minimizing human errors.
- **Improved Customer Experience:** Facilitates personalized services, proactive issue resolution, and remote monitoring, enhancing customer satisfaction.

Case Studies

- **Volkswagen Group:** Uses AWS IoT to improve vehicle connectivity and process real-time data, supporting smart mobility solutions and predictive maintenance.
- **iRobot:** Powers connected home devices through AWS IoT, enabling remote control, real-time updates, and smooth functionality for smart cleaning solutions.
- **Carrier:** Implements AWS IoT to optimize HVAC systems, improving energy efficiency and enabling predictive maintenance for both residential and commercial customers.

3.7 Sensor-Cloud: Sensors-as-a-Service

Sensing-as-a-Service (SaaS) provides a cloud-based framework that allows IoT devices to collect, process, and deliver sensor data efficiently. These systems are highly scalable, cost-effective, and capable of capturing data across large geographical areas, making them valuable for industries such as manufacturing, healthcare, logistics, and supply chain management. SaaS platforms simplify the process of gathering real-time information from connected sensors and transforming it into actionable insights. By providing data in a structured and understandable format, these systems help organizations optimize operations, monitor performance, and make informed decisions.

The IoT ecosystem is expanding rapidly, with the number of connected devices expected to reach tens of billions globally. Innovations in IoT are emerging continuously, introducing new applications, services, and technologies that push the boundaries of what is possible in data collection and analysis. In essence, Sensing-as-a-Service has become a critical enabler for businesses and developers looking to leverage IoT data effectively, offering a foundation for smarter, data-driven operations.

Sensing-as-a -Service in IoT architecture

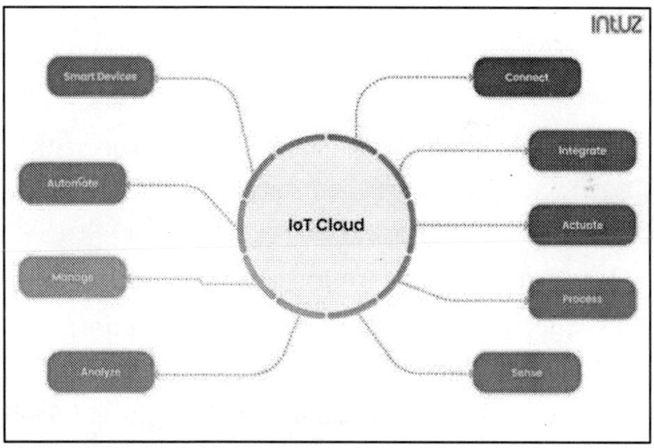

Fig. 3.15 SAAS Architecture

The key appeal of IoT lies in its potential to automate everyday activities seamlessly. For instance, consider having a perfectly brewed cup of coffee ready at the ideal time each morning. Determining the exact moment the coffee machine should start brewing could depend on several factors, such as:

- The time the alarm goes off
- The moment the person gets out of bed
- The time taken to reach the kitchen

Now, imagine a home equipped with sensors throughout the rooms, all connected to the coffee maker. **Sensing-as-a-Service (SaaS)** leverages these sensor networks and connected devices to provide real-time sensing capabilities.

To ensure secure and transparent exchange of sensor data, blockchain technology can be used during transmission. Meanwhile, the combination of cloud storage and common IoT infrastructure enables data to be efficiently collected, processed, and stored, all in a cost-effective manner.

Sensing-as-a-Service (SaaS) Model in the IoT Paradigm

To visualize the SaaS model in IoT, imagine it as a marketplace where sensor data acts as a platform. In this marketplace, data owners can share or sell their data to interested consumers, often following a **pay-as-you-go** approach.

A typical SaaS model in IoT consists of three main components:

1. **Sensing Devices** – Devices and sensors that collect real-time data from the environment or specific processes.
2. **Data Consumers** – Entities or users that require access to the sensor data for analysis, decision-making, or operational purposes.
3. **Sensing Infrastructure** – This includes service providers, servers, and publishers responsible for collecting, processing, and delivering the data to consumers.

In practice, the consumer submits a data request, and the service providers either gather the required information via sensing devices or retrieve it from existing databases. This sharing of IoT infrastructure significantly lowers the cost of acquiring sensor data, making it accessible to businesses of all sizes.

Architectural Requirements of a SaaS Model

- **Layered System Design** – The system must handle environmental and network changes efficiently and be optimized for low power consumption.
- **Device Abstraction** – Essential abstractions are required to enable basic operations across a wide variety of heterogeneous sensor devices.
- **Integration with Higher-Level Systems** – Seamless integration allows fast and consistent exchange of sensor data between systems.
- **Dynamic and Static Network Support** – The architecture should manage both fixed and mobile networks effectively.

Core Components

- **Worker Nodes** – Responsible for executing sensing tasks as instructed by the cloud platform.
- **Cloud Platform** – Oversees the entire sensing operation, coordinating data collection, processing, and distribution to consumers.

This setup ensures that sensor data can be efficiently collected, processed, and shared while minimizing infrastructure costs and maintaining flexibility for diverse IoT applications.

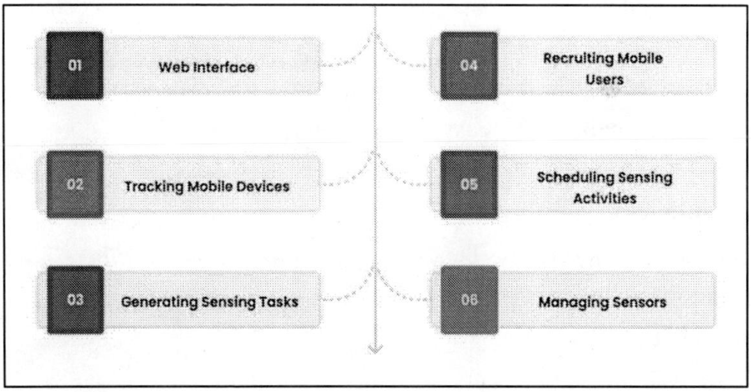

Fig. 3.16 Functionalities supported by the SaS model

Key Components of Sensing-as-a-Service (SaaS)

1. **Web Interface**: Acts as the main point of interaction for cloud users, allowing them to access information from anywhere using digital devices.

2. **Tracking Devices**: Maintains details about all network devices, including the number of sensors, their locations, battery levels, and mobile devices performing sensing tasks. A proper interface between mobile devices and sensing servers helps in collecting data and sending tasks to mobile devices.

3. **Task Generation**: Sensing tasks are created in response to user requests, ensuring that data collection aligns with user needs.

4. **Recruiting Mobile Users**: Service providers select mobile device users to participate in sensing activities according to the requirements of the sensing schedule.

5. **Scheduling Sensing Activities**: A scheduling algorithm or policy manages and monitors each sensing task, such as the transmission of data to the server and coordination with smart devices.

6. **Sensor Management**: Applications deployed on sensor devices allow them to perform the requested actions, including data collection and transmission to the server.

7. **Data Storage and Handling**: Data gathered by sensors is organized and stored in databases for easy retrieval and further analysis.

Advantages of Sensing-as-a-Service

SaaS offers significant benefits, especially in areas where timely information exchange is crucial for faster responses and effective incident management:

- **Real-Time Data Access:** Provides immediate access to sensor data, enabling quick decision-making.
- **Cost Efficiency:** Reduces the need for dedicated infrastructure as multiple users share sensor networks.
- **Scalability:** Easily integrates additional sensors or mobile devices

to meet growing data demands.

- **Flexibility:** Supports a variety of sensing tasks across different applications and domains.
- **Enhanced Responsiveness:** Helps organizations react promptly to events by supplying up-to-date and accurate data.

Advantages of Sensing-as-a-Service (SaS)

1. **Effective Performance in Challenging Environments**: Sensor networks can operate reliably in harsh or unsafe conditions, collecting data efficiently where manual efforts would be risky, slow, or costly.
2. **Scalability:** Sensor networks can easily expand or reduce the number of nodes to cover larger or smaller areas without upgrading existing sensors. This flexibility reduces costs while maintaining operational efficiency.
3. **Efficient Data Collection Across Wide Areas**: Sensors communicate via signal relays with other nodes in the network, enabling data collection over large geographic areas without requiring continuous connectivity throughout the network.
4. **Reduced Risk to Resources and Personnel**: By minimizing human involvement, sensors save labor hours and provide real-time and predictive information, helping to safeguard physical assets through timely interventions.
5. **Data Monetization**: Organizations can leverage existing sensor networks to generate new streams of valuable data, enabling real-time information to be converted into actionable insights or commercial value.

Disadvantages of Sensing-as-a-Service (SaS)

1. **Security Risks**: Since SaS is a relatively new technology, many sensor networks may lack strong security measures, making them vulnerable to attacks and unauthorized access.
2. **Energy Limitations**: Sensor devices are typically battery-powered, and limited battery life can lead to delays in network operations and

increased costs for routing or maintenance.

Key Use Cases of Sensing-as-a-Service (SaS)

IoT sensors are playing a crucial role in reducing operational costs, improving efficiency, and enhancing safety across industries. Here's how SaS is being applied in various sectors:

1. **Smart Cities**: Sensor networks are vital for the development of smart cities. They monitor traffic flow, parking availability, noise levels, and air pollution. Sensors also assess infrastructure health, allowing for timely preventive maintenance of bridges, buildings, and heritage sites. Moreover, connected sensors enable cost-efficient management of city utilities, including lighting, roads, and waste disposal.

2. **Smart Environment**: Environmental monitoring through smart sensors allows early detection of natural events and hazards. Sensors can detect earthquakes, forest fires via temperature changes, monitor snow levels to predict avalanches, and track soil conditions to prevent landslides. Additionally, air pollution levels can be monitored to regulate CO2 emissions effectively.

3. **Smart Water Management**: Sensors help track water quality in rivers, lakes, and reservoirs. They detect chemical leaks, pollution levels, and monitor dam water levels to prevent floods. At a local scale, sensors ensure proper water temperature and quality in pools and other water systems.

4. **Security Management**: Industrial and commercial sites benefit from sensors for security and emergency management. Perimeter access sensors detect unauthorized entry, while other sensors monitor radiation, liquid levels, and gas leaks to prevent accidents and ensure safety.

5. **Smart Logistics**: Supply chain operations are streamlined through sensors embedded in shipments and storage facilities. They help track inventory, monitor storage conditions, and maintain fleet health, optimizing vehicle usage and reducing operational risks.

6. **Industrial Management**: Factories use sensors to monitor

machinery health, floor conditions, and indoor air quality. Predictive maintenance through sensor data reduces manual checks and prevents mechanical failures. Advanced M2M (machine-to-machine) applications automate diagnostics, alerting operators to potential issues, controlling temperature, and detecting hazardous gas leaks.

Wireless Sensor Network (WSN)

A **Wireless Sensor Network (WSN)** is a decentralized network consisting of numerous wireless sensors deployed in an ad-hoc manner to monitor physical, environmental, or system conditions. Each sensor node contains a processor that collects and manages environmental data in its designated area.

The nodes communicate with a **Base Station**, which acts as the central processing unit for the network. The Base Station is typically connected to the Internet, allowing data to be processed, stored, analyzed, and shared. WSNs are widely used for environmental monitoring, industrial automation, smart infrastructure, and data-driven decision-making.

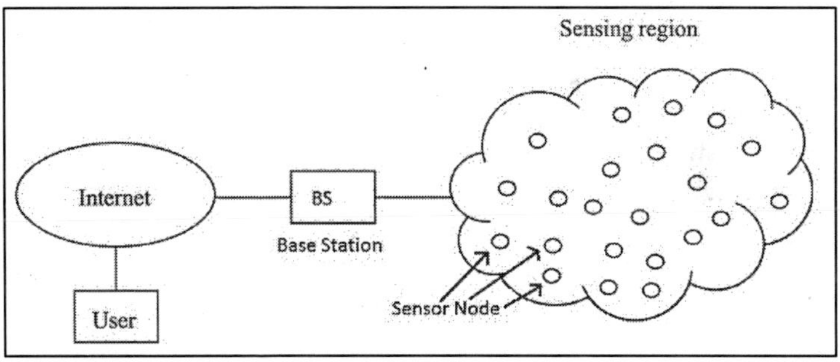

Fig. 3.17 WSN Architecture

Wireless Sensor Network (WSN) Architecture

A **Wireless Sensor Network (WSN)** is structured into three primary layers to facilitate efficient data collection and communication:

1. **Physical Layer**: This layer establishes the physical connection

between sensor nodes and the base station using technologies like radio waves, infrared, or Bluetooth. It ensures reliable signal transmission for node-to-node and node-to-base communication.

2. **Data Link Layer**: Responsible for providing a stable connection between nodes and the base station, this layer manages data transmission using protocols such as IEEE 802.15.4. It ensures efficient and reliable communication within the network.

3. **Application Layer**: This layer defines how sensor nodes transmit specific data to the base station. Protocols like ZigBee are used to structure and format data for various applications, including environmental monitoring, industrial control, and smart infrastructure management.

These layers work together to enable seamless operation and consistent data flow across the network.

WSN Network Topologies

Wireless Sensor Networks can be arranged in various topologies depending on the application and performance requirements:

1. **Bus Topology**: All nodes are connected along a single communication line (bus). Data travels sequentially from node to node. This simple layout is often used in smaller networks.

2. **Star Topology**: A central master node connects directly to multiple nodes. Communication occurs through the master node, making it ideal for centralized control and easy management.

3. **Tree Topology**: Nodes are organized hierarchically like branches of a tree. Data moves from child nodes to parent nodes along the branches. This topology helps expand coverage while maintaining organized communication.

4. **Mesh Topology**: Nodes are interconnected in a mesh-like structure, allowing data to travel via multiple paths to reach its destination. This topology provides redundancy, fault tolerance, and robust coverage.

The choice of topology depends on factors such as network size, coverage requirements, scalability, and reliability needs.

Types of Wireless Sensor Networks (WSN)

1. **Terrestrial WSNs**

- Deployed for communication between base stations on land.
- Consist of thousands of nodes arranged randomly (ad hoc) or in a planned manner.
- Often powered by solar cells to conserve energy.
- Focus on energy efficiency and optimized routing.

2. **Underground WSNs**

- Nodes are buried to monitor underground conditions.
- Require above-ground sink nodes for data transmission.
- Installation and maintenance are challenging and costly.
- Limited battery life due to difficulty in recharging.

3. **Underwater WSNs**

- Deployed in aquatic environments using sensor nodes and autonomous underwater vehicles (AUVs).
- Challenges include low data transmission rates, bandwidth limitations, and signal attenuation.
- Nodes are energy-constrained with non-rechargeable power sources.

4. **Multimedia WSNs**

- Designed to capture video, audio, and images for multimedia applications.
- Nodes are equipped with cameras and microphones.
- High power consumption and bandwidth requirements; complex data processing is needed.
- Efficient wireless data compression and transmission are critical.

5. **Mobile WSNs (MWSNs)**

- Composed of sensor nodes capable of independent movement.
- Offer increased coverage, improved energy efficiency, and higher channel capacity than static networks.
- Nodes can sense, compute, and communicate while moving, enabling dynamic monitoring.

Each type of WSN is tailored for specific environments and applications, leveraging appropriate technologies and strategies to ensure efficient sensing, communication, and data management.

Applications of Wireless Sensor Networks (WSN)

Wireless Sensor Networks (WSNs) are extensively used across various sectors due to their capability to monitor environments and collect data efficiently. Some prominent applications include:

- **Internet of Things (IoT):** WSNs act as the foundation for IoT ecosystems, allowing smart devices to communicate and exchange data seamlessly.
- **Surveillance and Security Monitoring:** WSNs support threat detection, intrusion monitoring, and safety surveillance in sensitive locations.
- **Environmental Monitoring:** These networks measure key environmental parameters, such as temperature, humidity, air pressure, and air quality.
- **Noise Monitoring:** Sensors track noise levels in urban areas, assisting in city planning and public health studies.
- **Healthcare:** WSNs enable patient monitoring, telemedicine, and remote health data collection.
- **Agriculture:** Sensor networks optimize crop management by monitoring soil moisture, nutrient levels, and climate conditions.
- **Disaster Detection:** WSNs provide early warnings for natural hazards like landslides, floods, and earthquakes.

Challenges in Wireless Sensor Networks

While WSNs offer significant advantages, they also face technical and operational challenges, including:

1. **Energy and Power Constraints:** Most sensor nodes rely on batteries, limiting operational lifespan. Effective energy management is critical to ensure long-term functionality.

2. **Limited Processing and Storage:** Sensor nodes often have restricted computing power and storage, making it difficult to handle complex tasks or large datasets.

3. **Heterogeneity:** Networks often include various sensor types and nodes with different capabilities, complicating integration and management.

4. **Security Threats:** WSNs are susceptible to attacks such as eavesdropping, jamming, spoofing, and unauthorized access. Ensuring secure data transmission and network protection is essential.

5. **Scalability Issues:** The network must accommodate large numbers of nodes and manage significant data volumes without affecting performance.

6. **Interference:** External wireless signals can disrupt communication between nodes, impacting network reliability.

7. **Reliability and Fault Tolerance:** For critical applications, WSNs must maintain accurate data collection and continue functioning despite node failures.

8. **Quality of Service (QoS) and Performance:** Ensuring high throughput, low latency, and effective cross-layer optimization is a continuous challenge for WSN deployment.

WSNs are indispensable for real-time monitoring and data collection. However, addressing these challenges is crucial for their successful deployment in large-scale and mission-critical environments.

Components of Wireless Sensor Networks (WSN)

Wireless Sensor Networks consist of several key components that work together to collect, transmit, and process environmental data:

1. **Sensors:** Sensors capture environmental variables such as temperature, humidity, or pressure. The physical signals they detect are converted into electrical signals for processing.

2. **Radio Nodes:** These nodes receive data from the sensors and transmit it wirelessly to the WLAN access point. Each node typically

includes a microcontroller, transceiver, external memory, and a power source.

3. **WLAN Access Point:** The access point collects data sent by the radio nodes and transmits it over the Internet for further processing and storage.

4. **Evaluation Software:** This software processes the data collected from sensors and presents it in a meaningful format. It enables further analysis, storage, and mining to support decision-making and reporting.

Advantages of WSN

- **Cost-Effective:** Small, low-cost sensors make WSNs affordable and easy to deploy.
- **Wireless Communication:** Eliminates the need for costly wired connections, allowing flexible network deployment.
- **Energy Efficiency:** Low-power devices and protocols extend operational lifetime without frequent battery replacements.
- **Scalability:** Sensors can be added or removed easily, making WSNs suitable for small- to large-scale deployments.
- **Real-Time Monitoring:** Provides timely data for decision-making, control, and environmental monitoring.

Disadvantages of WSN

- **Limited Range:** Wireless communication can be restricted by distance and physical obstacles.
- **Limited Processing Power:** Low-power devices often have restricted computational capabilities and memory.
- **Security Risks:** Vulnerable to attacks like eavesdropping, tampering, and denial-of-service, which can compromise data integrity.
- **Interference:** Data transmission may be affected by interference from other wireless devices or environmental noise.
- **Deployment Challenges:** Proper sensor placement, power management, and network configuration can be time-consuming and

resource-intensive.

While WSNs provide many benefits, these limitations must be addressed for effective real-world deployment.

Sensor Cloud Architecture

The **Sensor Cloud Architecture** can be understood from two perspectives:

1. **User and Organizational View:** Focuses on outcomes, usability, and the seamless integration of sensor data into applications and business processes. Users care about real-time insights, analytics, and ease of access.

2. **Technical Implementation View:** Emphasizes the underlying infrastructure, including layered architecture, virtualization, data storage, and processing. This view involves managing large-scale sensor networks, ensuring reliability, and maintaining secure and efficient data flow.

Sensor cloud platforms essentially virtualize WSNs and make their data accessible on-demand,

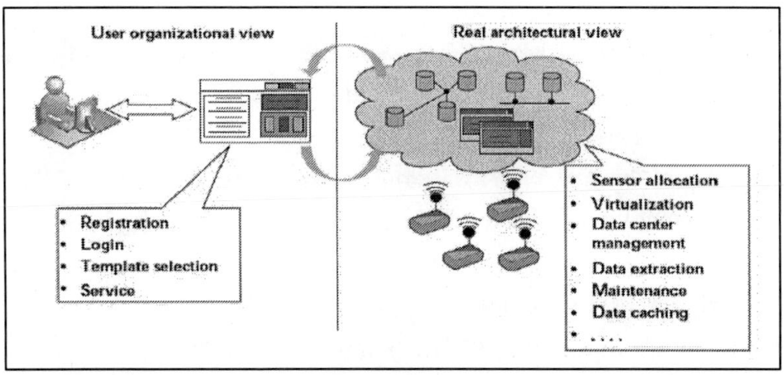

Fig. 3.18 Sensor-Cloud Architecture Perspective

User/Organizational Viewpoint: Sensing-as-a-Service (Se-aaS)

From a **user or organizational perspective**, the Se-aaS architecture is designed as a flexible, easy-to-use platform that abstracts the complexities of physical sensors, allowing seamless access to sensing capabilities.

Key Features:

- **Abstraction and Virtualization:** Users interact with virtual sensors or service instances via web interfaces or APIs, without needing knowledge of the physical sensor's location, type, or technical details.
- **Focus on Outcomes:** The main objective is the reliable delivery of sensor data for applications such as environmental monitoring, healthcare, or asset tracking, supporting informed decision-making and business operations.

Benefits:

1. **Scalability:** Resources can be scaled up or down dynamically without investing in physical infrastructure.
2. **Cost-Effectiveness:** Reduces costs related to sensor maintenance, deployment, and operational management.
3. **Collaboration and Sharing:** Enables data sharing across multiple users and applications, enhancing resource utilization and cross-disciplinary projects.
4. **Dynamic Provisioning:** Allows on-demand allocation and release of sensor resources based on current requirements.

Real Architectural View: Layered Infrastructure

The **technical architecture** of Se-aaS involves a multi-layered system that manages and delivers sensor data efficiently. This is typically structured into three main layers:

1. Sensor-Centric Layer (Infrastructure Layer)

- **Components:** Physical sensors (temperature, GPS, image, etc.), actuators, and communication protocols like Zigbee, Wi-Fi, or cellular, connected to IoT gateways.
- **Functionality:**
  - Captures raw sensor data.
  - Performs initial data processing.

- Secures and transmits data to the cloud infrastructure via gateways.

2. Sensor Cloud / Middleware Layer (Control & Service Management Layer)

- **Components:**
  - **Virtualization Manager:** Maps physical sensors to virtual sensors and creates virtual sensor groups per user requests.
  - **Data Management:** Handles storage, caching, and large-scale data processing.
  - **Service Management:** Manages user requests, security, Quality of Service (QoS), and data routing to applications.
  - **Service Templates:** Predefined templates to automatically generate specific service instances.
- **Functionality:**
  - Translates generic user commands into specific instructions for physical sensors.
  - Controls data flow and ensures efficient resource utilization.
  - Provides abstraction for users, hiding the complexity of physical hardware.

3. Application/Client-Centric Layer

- **Components:** Web portals, mobile applications, enterprise servers, and analysis tools.
- **Functionality:**
  - Provides data visualization and advanced analytics.
  - Enables user interaction and integration with business processes.
  - Delivers actionable insights powered by the underlying sensor data.

This layered approach ensures that **Se-aaS platforms provide seamless, scalable, and secure access** to sensor data, while hiding the complexity of hardware and network management from end-users.

A **traditional Wireless Sensor Network (WSN)** is primarily designed for a single user or a specific application, where sensors are dedicated to collecting and transmitting data for that purpose. In contrast, a **sensor cloud** is built on cloud computing principles and integrates multiple WSNs to provide shared services to multiple users. Unlike a WSN, which is focused on data collection for a single application, a sensor cloud is service-oriented, offering virtualization of sensors and enabling resource sharing across diverse applications and users. This makes sensor clouds more flexible, scalable, and capable of supporting a wider range of services than traditional WSNs.

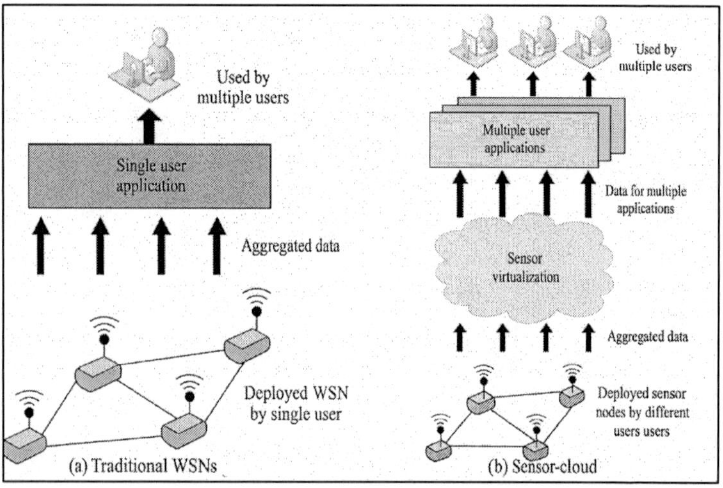

Fig. 3.19 Traditional WSN v/s Sensor-cloud

Lets understand the case by real time examples:

Traditional Wireless Sensor Network (WSN) Example: Soil Moisture Monitoring System

Scenario

A farmer wants to keep track of soil moisture levels across a large agricultural field to optimize irrigation and reduce water waste.

Components

- **Sensor Nodes:** Compact, battery-operated units equipped with soil moisture sensors, microcontrollers, and low-power wireless modules (such as LoRaWAN). These are distributed throughout the field.

- **Gateway/Base Station:** A central device that receives moisture readings from all sensor nodes. It then forwards this information through the internet to a local server or monitoring system.
- **Local Server / Monitoring Dashboard:** Displays simple moisture readings—like *dry*, *moist*, or *wet*. It can also generate alerts to the farmer's mobile phone for irrigation decisions.

Function

Each node measures the soil moisture and transmits the data wirelessly to the gateway. The gateway sends the collected information to the server. The system provides real-time monitoring with minimal power use because most processing happens locally.

Sensor Cloud Example: Smart City Air Quality Monitoring

Scenario

A smart city needs real-time air pollution insights across various locations to support health alerts, urban planning, and environmental policies.

Components

- **Distributed WSNs:** Sensor nodes installed on street poles, rooftops, and public vehicles that measure air pollutants like PM2.5, CO, and NO_2.
- **Cloud Platform (AWS, Azure, etc.):** Responsible for handling high-volume sensor data. It provides services like:
    - IoT data ingestion
    - Large-scale storage
    - Data analytics and machine learning
    - APIs for external applications
- **Web and Mobile Applications:** Allow users to view interactive pollution heatmaps, past trends, real-time levels, and receive health-related recommendations based on air quality.

Function

Sensor nodes send continuous environmental data to the cloud. The cloud processes and analyzes the data to identify pollution levels, detect hotspots, and forecast future air quality. This information is then accessible to citizens, government departments, and health experts via apps and dashboards.

3.8 Difference Between WSN and Sensor-Cloud

Table 3.2

Feature	Traditional Wireless Sensor Network (WSN)	Sensor Cloud
Architecture	A dedicated network of sensors, often with a central sink or base station.	A cloud-computing infrastructure that integrates one or more WSNs, allowing for greater scalability and shared resources.
User Focus	Single-user or single-application centric, collecting data for a specific purpose.	Multi-user and multi-application, enabling various users and applications to access and share sensor data from multiple networks.
Service Model	Data-centric, providing a dedicated data-gathering service.	Service-centric, offering "Sensors-as-a-Service" (Se-aaS) and virtualizing physical sensors into virtual ones for multiple users.
Connectivity	No direct internet connection; data is	Direct or near-direct connection to the internet

	routed to a local gateway or router for processing and distribution.	via a gateway, allowing for remote access and cloud integration.
Scalability	Limited scalability; a network is typically built for a specific purpose and cannot easily accommodate numerous, diverse applications.	High scalability due to the cloud infrastructure, which can handle the demands of many users and applications simultaneously.

Exercise

MCQs (Multiple Choice Questions)

1. Which of the following is a key benefit of cloud computing for IoT?

a) High local processing cost

b) Scalable storage and processing

c) Limited device connectivity

d) Manual data management

Answer: b) Scalable storage and processing

2. Virtualization in cloud computing allows:

a) Running multiple virtual machines on a single physical machine

b) Direct physical data storage only

c) Reducing sensor sensitivity

d) Hardware replacement automatically

Answer: a) Running multiple virtual machines on a single physical machine

3. Which of the following is not a cloud deployment model?

a) Public Cloud

b) Private Cloud

c) Hybrid Cloud

d) Local Cloud

Answer: d) Local Cloud

4. SLA (Service-Level Agreement) in cloud computing defines:

a) Hardware color preferences

b) The expected level of service and performance metrics

c) Cloud provider marketing strategy

d) Device battery usage

Answer: b) The expected level of service and performance metrics

5. Sensors-as-a-Service (Sensor-Cloud) mainly provides:

a) Physical sensors for free

b) Access to sensor data and processing over the cloud

c) Local data storage only

d) Device manufacturing guidelines

Answer: b) Access to sensor data and processing over the cloud

Very Short Answer Questions

1. What is cloud computing in the context of IoT?

2. Define virtualization in cloud computing.

3. Name the three main cloud deployment models.

4. What is the purpose of an SLA in cloud computing?

5. What does Sensor-Cloud or Sensors-as-a-Service provide to IoT users?

Short Answer Questions

1. Explain the difference between public, private, and hybrid cloud models.

2. What are the advantages of using cloud computing in IoT systems?

3. How does virtualization support efficient resource utilization in the cloud?

4. Describe the role of SLA in maintaining cloud service quality.

5. How does Sensor-Cloud facilitate data collection and analytics for IoT applications?

Long Answer Questions

1. Discuss cloud computing concepts and its importance in IoT applications. Include examples of IoT scenarios that benefit from cloud computing.

2. Explain the different cloud deployment models (public, private, hybrid) and their suitability for IoT projects.

3. Describe virtualization in cloud computing, its advantages, and how it enhances IoT system efficiency.

4. Explain the role of Service-Level Agreements (SLA) in cloud computing and why they are critical for IoT service providers.

5. Discuss the concept of Sensor-Cloud or Sensors-as-a-Service, including its architecture, working, and benefits in IoT ecosystems.

Unit-4

IOT CASE STUDIES AND FUTURE TRENDS

4.1 Vehicular IoT-Introduction and Case Studies

Introduction:

The rapid growth in the number of vehicles has led to challenges such as traffic congestion and parking management. The Internet of Things (IoT) has enabled the development of connected vehicular systems that improve the efficiency of transportation networks. Vehicular IoT extends to various areas of transportation, including traffic management on roads, driver safety for both large and small vehicles, and security in public transit. In a connected environment, vehicles can communicate with each other and share data, allowing them to sense their internal and external surroundings and make autonomous decisions. Additionally, IoT infrastructure allows vehicle owners to monitor and track their vehicles easily.

Architecture of Vehicular IoT: The architecture of Vehicular IoT is structured into three layers: Device, Fog, and Cloud.

1. **Device Layer:** This is the foundational layer of the system. It comprises the vehicles and roadside units (RSUs). Vehicles are equipped with sensors that collect data about the vehicle's internal status, while RSUs act as localized control units to manage and process data from the vehicles.

2. **Fog Layer:** The fog layer provides intermediate processing close to the devices, enabling faster decision-making. This is critical for avoiding accidents and improving traffic flow by processing data locally before it reaches the cloud.

3. **Cloud Layer:** The cloud layer handles large-scale data storage, advanced analytics, and long-term decision-making. It integrates data

from multiple fog nodes to provide insights, optimize traffic management, and support vehicle tracking and predictive maintenance.

This layered approach ensures efficient data collection, processing, and actionable insights, enhancing vehicle safety, traffic management, and overall transportation efficiency.

Fog computing plays a crucial role by providing decisions in real-time.

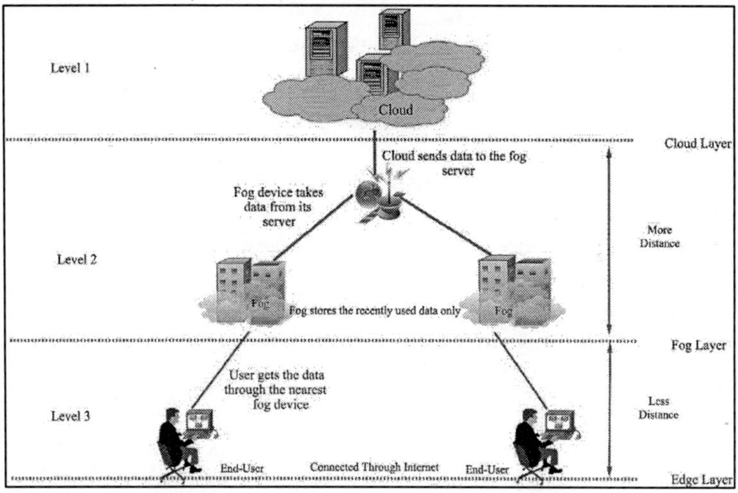

Fig. 4.1 Architecture of Vehicular IoT Layers

Difference between Edge Computing, Fog Computing and Cloud Computing

Table 4.1

Feature	Edge Computing	Fog Computing	Cloud Computing
Data Processing Location	Directly on the end-user device or sensor.	In a network layer (fog nodes) between the edge and cloud.	In large, centralized data centers, often far from the data source.

Latency	Lowest (immediate).	Low (faster than cloud).	High (slower response times).
Bandwidth	Lowest requirement (most processing is local).	Moderate requirement (filters and aggregates data before sending to cloud).	Highest requirement (sends all raw data).
Processing Power	Limited by the device's capabilities.	More powerful than individual edge devices, but less than the cloud.	Highest capacity for large-scale processing and long-term storage.
Security	High (data can be kept local).	Medium (data is aggregated at fog nodes but is still distributed).	Can be lower (data travels over networks).
Best For	Tasks needing instant responses, such as real-time analytics on a single device or machine vision.	Collaborating across multiple edge devices or situations that need local, real-time analysis before sending data to the cloud.	Large-scale data analysis, long-term data storage, and tasks that can tolerate higher latency.

Components of vehicular IoT

The main components of vehicular IoT include sensors, communication technology, processing units, and the cloud or fog infrastructure. Internal vehicle sensors monitor performance, while external sensors and cameras gather environmental data. Wireless connectivity enables data transmission from the vehicle to roadside units (RSUs) and then to the cloud for processing and decision-making. Vehicular IoT systems are composed of several integral components that work together to enable connected, intelligent, and safe transportation:

1. **Sensors:**

Sensors are the primary data collection devices in vehicles and are divided into:

- **Internal Sensors:** Monitor the vehicle's own performance, including engine status, fuel levels, tire pressure, and speed.
- **External Sensors and Cameras:** Gather information about the surrounding environment, such as road conditions, nearby vehicles, pedestrians, and obstacles.

Table 4.2

Feature	Internal Sensors	External Sensors
Purpose	Monitor an object's internal condition and status.	Monitor and measure the external environment or objects outside the device.
Examples	Temperature monitors, strain gauges, pressure sensors, and position encoders within a device.	Air quality sensors, cameras, light sensors, and GPS receivers that interact with the outside world.
Interaction	Provide data about the device's own	Provide data about the device's surroundings,

	dynamics, like its power consumption or physical stress.	like the temperature of a room or the presence of a person.
Maintenance	Can simplify maintenance as they are protected inside the device.	May require more maintenance, such as external cleaning or recalibration, depending on the sensor type.

2. **Communication:** Wireless connectivity allows vehicles to transmit and receive data in real time. Common connectivity technologies include Wi-Fi, Bluetooth, and cellular networks like GSM and 5G.

3. **Roadside Units (RSUs):** RSUs act as local communication hubs installed along roads. They collect data from vehicles and other infrastructure components, relay information to nearby vehicles, and transmit it to higher-level systems for processing.

4. **Processing Units:**

   - **On-board Processing:** Vehicle-mounted processors analyze sensor data locally to enable immediate responses, such as braking or lane adjustments.

   - **Fog/Edge Computing:** Processing occurs closer to the data source, often at RSUs, to reduce latency and allow faster decision-making compared to sending all data to the cloud.

5. **Cloud Infrastructure:** The cloud serves as a centralized hub for storing and analyzing large volumes of data.

   - **Data Storage:** Maintains historical data for long-term analysis.

   - **Advanced Analytics:** Performs complex computations, predictive modeling, and decision-making that require high computational resources beyond local processing.

6. **Satellites:**

Satellites provide geolocation services, vehicle tracking, crash detection, and road condition monitoring through satellite imagery.

Advantages of Vehicular IoT

Vehicular IoT provides several benefits that improve vehicle management, safety, and connectivity:

1. **Easy Tracking:** Vehicles can be monitored in real-time, allowing the system to identify the location and status of each vehicle, even from remote locations.
2. **Fast Decision Making:** By leveraging cloud and fog computing, vehicular IoT enables rapid data processing from sensors, allowing quick responses to avoid accidents and traffic hazards.
3. **Connected Vehicles:** Vehicles can communicate and share information with each other, enhancing traffic coordination and situational awareness.
4. **Efficient Management:** With integrated sensors, communication units, processing devices, and GPS systems, vehicular IoT allows seamless management of multiple vehicles and users spread across various geographic locations.
5. **Enhanced Safety:** Internal and external sensors continuously monitor vehicle and environmental conditions, ensuring the safety of occupants, pedestrians, and surrounding vehicles.
6. **Data Recording:** Vehicular IoT systems maintain detailed records, including video footage, images, and other documentation. Cloud and fog infrastructure ensures that this data is stored and accessible for analysis and future reference.

Crime Assistance in Smart IoT Transportation Systems

A notable application of vehicular IoT is enhancing public safety through intelligent crime detection. The **Fog-based Framework for Intelligent Public Safety in Vehicular Environments (Fog-FISVER)** is designed to improve safety in public transport, such as buses, through real-time surveillance and rapid reporting.

Key Steps of Fog-FISVER:

1. **Smart Surveillance in Vehicles:** Vehicles are equipped with

cameras and sensors capable of detecting criminal activity in real-time.

2. **Fog Computing Mediator:** A fog computing layer acts as an intermediary between the vehicle and police units, processing data locally to reduce response times.

3. **Mobile Crime Reporting:** A dedicated mobile application enables quick reporting of criminal activities to nearby law enforcement agents.

Three-Tiered Architecture of Fog-FISVER:

- **Tier 1:** Collects and processes raw data from within the vehicle to detect potential criminal activities. It generates crime-level metadata and sends it to the next tier.
  - **Image Processor:** Handles video and image data to detect suspicious activity.
  - **Event Dispatcher:** Transfers relevant information and alerts to higher-level processing or authorities.

This architecture demonstrates how vehicular IoT, combined with fog and cloud computing, can enhance safety and crime prevention in smart transportation systems.

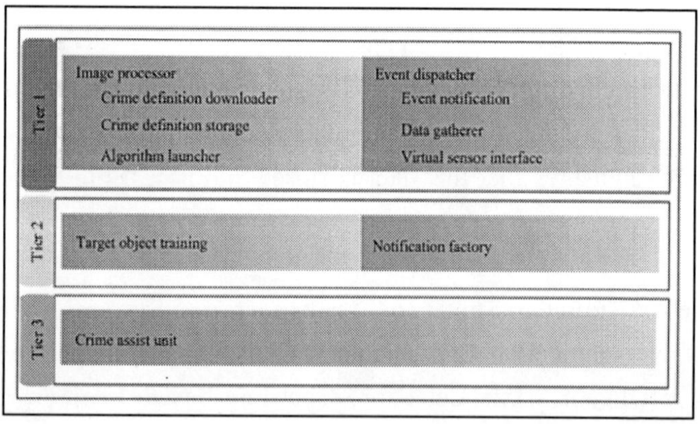

Fig. 4.2 Three-Tiered Architecture of Fog-FISVER

Image Processor in Vehicular IoT (Fog-FISVER)

The **Image Processor** in the Fog-FISVER framework is responsible for analyzing visual data to detect criminal activity in real-time. Key aspects include:

- **Deep Learning-Based Processing:** Developers employ deep learning techniques to enhance image analysis, allowing accurate recognition of suspicious objects or activities.
- **Hardware Platform:** A **Raspberry Pi 3** board is used, equipped with a high-resolution camera to capture real-time images and video within the vehicle.
- **Crime Object Templates:** The processor maintains a set of predefined crime-related object templates stored in the fog layer. These templates are used to compare and identify potential threats or criminal behavior efficiently.

This combination of AI-driven processing and edge computing ensures rapid detection and minimal delay in alerting authorities about security incidents.

• This has mainly three parts:

Table 4.3

a) Crime definition downloader	(b) Crime definition storage	(c) Algorithm launcher:
This checks for presence of new crime object template definitions in fog.	The crime definition storage is used to store all the possible crime object template definitions.	This is used to match the template with the video captured by the camera.

Event Dispatcher in Vehicular IoT (Fog-FISVER)

The **Event Dispatcher** plays a critical role in the Fog-FISVER framework by managing and routing data collected from vehicles and the image processor. Its main responsibilities include aggregating real-time information, generating alerts, and forwarding relevant data to higher tiers for further action.

Key Components of the Event Dispatcher:

1. **Data Aggregator:** Collects and organizes data received from the vehicle's sensors and the image processor, ensuring it is structured for

analysis.

2. Event Analyzer: Evaluates the aggregated data to identify suspicious or abnormal activities based on predefined rules or patterns.

3. Alert Generator: Generates real-time notifications or metadata when a potential crime or abnormal event is detected.

4. Data Forwarder: Transmits the processed information and alerts to the next tier in the fog computing architecture, such as the police or control center.

By efficiently managing and distributing sensed data, the Event Dispatcher ensures timely responses and enhances public safety in the smart vehicular IoT ecosystem.

Table 4.4

(a) Event notifier	(b) Data gatherer	(c) Virtual sensor interface
It transfers the data to the fog-FISVER STS fog infrastructure	This is an intermediate component between the event notifier and the physical sensor; it helps to gather sensed data	The virtual sensor interface helps to maintain a particular procedure to gather data. This component also cooperates to register the sensors in the system.

Tier 2 — FISVER STS Fog Infrastructure

Tier 2 of the Fog-FISVER architecture acts as the intelligent middle layer that connects vehicles with law enforcement units. It performs crucial analysis and coordination functions to enhance public safety in smart transportation systems.

This tier is responsible for three major tasks:

- **Updating object templates:** Continuously refreshes and maintains the database of crime-related object templates to ensure accurate detection.
- **Event classification:** Analyzes the metadata received from Tier 1 to categorize events based on severity and type.
- **Police unit selection:** Identifies and selects the most appropriate police vehicle or officer to receive alerts, based on proximity and availability.

To manage these operations effectively, the FISVER STS fog layer is divided into two major sub-components, each designed to handle specialized processing and decision-making functions.

Table 4.5

Target Object Training	Notification Factory
creating, updating, and storing the crime object definition	This sub-component receives notification about the events in a different vehicle with the installed system.

(iii) Tier 3 — Mobile Application Layer

Tier 3 represents the topmost layer in the FISVER architecture and consists of mobile applications installed on users' smartphones. These applications enable passengers or bystanders to report suspicious or criminal activities directly to nearby police personnel. This layer empowers citizens to participate in improving public safety by providing real-time alerts through an easy-to-use interface.

4.2 Healthcare IoT-Introduction and Case Studies

IoT technology has transformed the healthcare sector by introducing intelligent devices and systems that continuously monitor and analyze human health conditions. These IoT-enabled solutions are widely used for disease diagnosis, remote health tracking, and caring for elderly individuals, children, and infants.

IoT-based healthcare platforms significantly enhance the overall quality of life by providing timely access to vital health information. Through portable smart devices, users can monitor their physiological parameters, stay informed about potential health risks, and take preventive actions to avoid certain illnesses.

Specialized sensors embedded in these systems are designed to accurately capture and measure a variety of human physiological signals. They help in early detection, ongoing monitoring, and efficient medical decision-making.

These IoT healthcare systems typically operate through **four distinct layers**, each responsible for data collection, transmission, processing, and service delivery.

Layer 1: Perception Layer (Sensing Layer)

This is the lowest layer of Healthcare IoT.

Role:

- Collects raw data from the patient or environment.

Components:

- Body sensors (ECG, temperature, blood pressure, glucose monitor, pulse oximeter)
- Wearable devices (smartwatches, fitness bands)
- Implantable sensors (pacemakers, insulin pumps)
- Environmental sensors (room temperature, humidity, motion)

What it does:

- Detects physical, physiological, or environmental parameters
- Converts them into digital signals for transmission

Layer 2: Network Layer (Communication Layer)

Role:

- Transfers data from sensors to gateways, servers, or cloud platforms.

Technologies used:

- Wi-Fi, Bluetooth, BLE, ZigBee
- 4G/5G, LTE-M, NB-IoT
- RFID, NFC
- Medical Body Area Networks (MBAN)

What it does:

- Ensures reliable and secure data transmission
- Handles routing between devices and backend systems

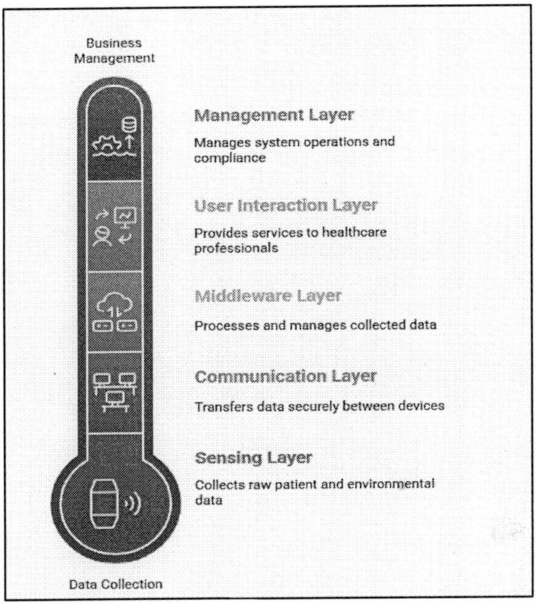

Fig. 4.3 Layers of Healthcare IOT

Layer 3: Cloud or High-End Server Layer (Middleware/Cloud Layer)

Role:

- Processes and manages the data collected from patients.

Components / Technologies:

- Cloud servers (AWS, Azure, Google Cloud)
- Fog/Edge computing systems
- Databases and big data frameworks

Functions:

- Data aggregation and filtering
- Analytics and machine learning
- Storage and retrieval of health records
- Ensures interoperability between devices and apps

Layer 4: User Interaction Layer.Application Layer

Role:

- Provides end-user services to doctors, patients, hospitals, and caregivers.

Examples:

- Remote patient monitoring dashboards
- Telemedicine apps
- Emergency alert systems
- Smart ICU monitoring
- Health data visualization apps

What it does:

- Converts processed data into meaningful insights
- Supports clinical decision-making

5. Business Layer (Management Layer)

Role:

- Manages the entire IoT system from an operational and business viewpoint.

Functions:

- Healthcare workflow management
- Billing, insurance integration
- Data privacy and compliance (HIPAA, GDPR)
- Access control and user management
- Evaluation of system performance
- Planning and policy-making

Components of Healthcare IoT

1. Sensors

The first layer primarily consists of medical and physiological sensors that capture patient-specific health data. These sensors measure various parameters such as:

- Blood oxygen level (SpO_2)
- Heart rate
- Airflow
- Body temperature

These sensors gather real-time physiological signals essential for continuous health monitoring.

2. Wireless Connectivity

Connectivity ensures seamless communication between different components of the system.

- **Sensor to Local Processing Unit (LPU):** Data is transmitted either through wired links or wireless technologies like Bluetooth and Zigbee.
- **LPU to Cloud/Server:** Long-distance communication uses the Internet via Wi-Fi, WLAN, or similar networking technologies. This ensures that the processed or raw data reaches cloud platforms for deeper analysis and storage.

3. Privacy and Security

Healthcare data is extremely sensitive. Any unauthorized access, loss, or theft of medical records can lead to serious legal and ethical issues. To prevent such risks, healthcare systems implement strong security measures including:

- Data encryption
- Secure authentication
- Access control policies

These practices safeguard patient information at every step of data transmission and storage.

4. Analytics

Analytics plays a crucial role in converting raw sensor data into meaningful medical insights.

It helps:

- Doctors and nurses access health information in customized formats
- Identify trends or abnormalities in patient data
- Diagnose diseases using the processed physiological signals

Analytics transforms basic data into actionable knowledge.

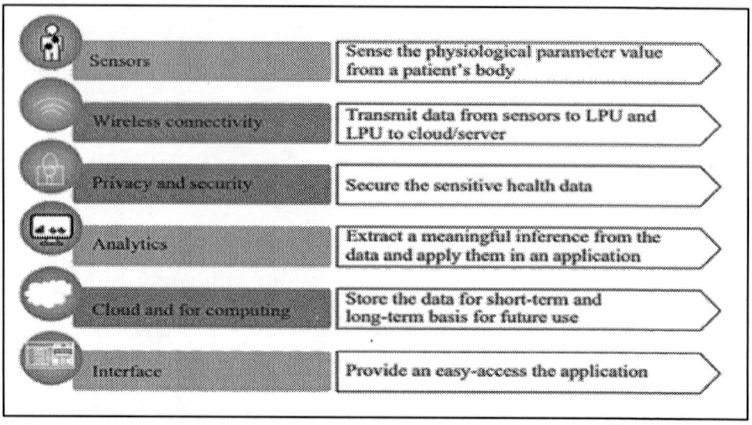

Fig. 4.4 Components of Healthcare IOT

(v) Cloud and Fog Computing

Sensors in a healthcare IoT environment generate large volumes of diverse physiological data. Cloud and fog computing help store, manage, and analyze this information efficiently.

- **Cloud storage** provides scalable space where patient records, medical histories, and long-term health data can be kept securely.
- Since cloud services follow a pay-as-you-use model, hospitals and healthcare organizations can expand storage as needed without heavy upfront investment.
- Both cloud and fog layers support advanced processing, enabling disease diagnosis, patient monitoring, and prediction of future health conditions.

(vi) Interface

The interface is the user-facing component of a healthcare IoT system and plays a crucial role in accessibility.

A well-designed interface should:

- Display health information clearly
- Present data in an easy-to-read, meaningful format
- Adapt or restructure information when required for better

understanding

This ensures that patients, doctors, and medical staff can easily interpret the data and take appropriate actions.

Advantages of Healthcare IoT

1. Real-Time Monitoring

Healthcare IoT systems provide instant updates to all stakeholders—doctors, patients, and hospital staff.

- Doctors can remotely monitor a patient's health in real time and offer quick medical advice when needed.
- Hospital staff gain visibility into current operational details, such as:
  - Number of patients admitted
  - Availability of beds and doctors
  - Overall activity and revenue of the healthcare unit

Real-time access significantly improves decision-making and patient care.

2. Low Cost

Healthcare IoT reduces unnecessary expenses and effort:

- Authorized users can check bed availability or facility status using an Internet connection and a simple browser.
- There is no need for physical visits to gather basic information.

This leads to time and cost savings for both patients and hospitals.

3. Easy Management

IoT-driven healthcare systems simplify the management of various components such as:

- Users and patients
- Medical devices
- Hospital facilities
- Costs and billing
- Security policies

With centralized monitoring and automation, healthcare units can run more efficiently with fewer errors.

4. Automatic Processing

Using IoT, many hospital processes can be automated from start to finish.

Examples include:

- Patient registration
- Record updates
- Treatment monitoring
- Discharge procedures

The system integrates information across all departments, resulting in a smooth and quick workflow across the entire healthcare chain.

5. Easy Record-Keeping

Healthcare facilities must maintain detailed records of their operations, medical activities, and financial transactions for future planning and improvement. Healthcare IoT systems help store such information securely in digital form. These records can be accessed by authorized personnel at any time, ensuring transparency, accuracy, and efficient management.

6. Easy Diagnosis

IoT-based healthcare systems simplify the diagnosis process by using advanced analytical tools and machine learning techniques. With access to historical health data and real-time physiological information, healthcare professionals can detect symptoms earlier and identify diseases more accurately. This reduces the chances of misdiagnosis and improves patient outcomes.

Risks in Healthcare IoT

1. Loss of Connectivity

Healthcare IoT systems rely heavily on stable Internet connectivity. Any interruption may lead to missing or delayed patient data, which could be life-threatening in critical situations. Therefore, continuous, reliable network availability is essential.

2. Security Concerns

Medical information is highly sensitive and must remain confidential. However, IoT systems are vulnerable to cyber threats such as unauthorized access, data tampering, and hacking. Any breach can expose patient data and cause severe legal and ethical issues.

3. Errors in Data

IoT systems handle massive amounts of physiological data. Even small errors in data collection or transmission may lead to incorrect analysis, misinterpretation of symptoms, or wrong diagnosis. Maintaining data accuracy and quality is a major challenge.

Case Study – AmbuSens System

The **AmbuSens** system was developed by the *Smart Wireless Applications and Networking (SWAN) Laboratory* at the **Indian Institute of Technology (IIT) Kharagpur**, with support from the **Ministry of Human Resource Development (MHRD)**, Government of India.

Objective

AmbuSens aims to enable **real-time remote monitoring of patients during ambulance transit**. It helps hospital staff assess the patient's condition before arrival, prepare necessary equipment, and provide faster, more effective treatment—potentially saving lives.

Key Features of the AmbuSens System

1. Continuous Monitoring

A **Wireless Body Area Network (WBAN)** consisting of multiple sensors, such as ECG, SpO_2, EMG, temperature, and GSR sensors, collects a patient's vital signs continuously.

2. Real-Time Data Transmission

Collected data is transmitted to the cloud through **Wi-Fi, 3G, or 4G networks**, ensuring that hospital personnel receive updates instantly.

3. Improved Hospital Preparedness

Doctors and medical staff can log into a web interface to view patient data in real time. This helps them prepare equipment, medication, and specialists before the patient reaches the hospital.

4. Remote Medical Guidance

Doctors at the hospital can communicate with paramedics inside the ambulance, providing immediate instructions based on the live data.

5. Data Security and Privacy

To protect patient confidentiality, the system uses a **hash-based privacy mechanism**. Each patient is assigned a frequently changing hash value, ensuring anonymity during data transmission and storage.

6. Location Tracking

Built-in GPS allows hospitals to track the ambulance's movement and estimate the arrival time accurately.

AmbuSens Architecture

Layer 1 – WBAN Layer

This layer includes multiple sensors attached to the patient's body. These sensors gather physiological data and send it to the next layer.

Layer 2 – Cloud Layer

Layer 2 handles cloud-based storage and processing.

- WBANs from different patients send large volumes of data.
- The cloud uses **big data analytics** to analyze this information in real time.

Layer 3 – Privacy & Security Layer

All hashing operations occur at this layer. A new hash value is generated at different time intervals, ensuring that patient identity remains anonymous.

Layer 4 – User Layer

Authorized users, such as doctors, hospital staff, and paramedics, register themselves and access the system as needed.

Hardware Components in AmbuSens

Sensors

The WBAN includes:

- Optical pulse sensor

- ECG unit
- EMG sensor
- Temperature sensor
- GSR (Galvanic Skin Response) sensor

These sensors continuously monitor the patient's physiological conditions.

Local Data Processing Unit (LDPU)

The LDPU is a compact processing board with limited computing power.

- It collects data from all WBAN sensors.
- It performs basic preprocessing.
- It sends the processed data to the cloud for deeper analysis and long-term storage.

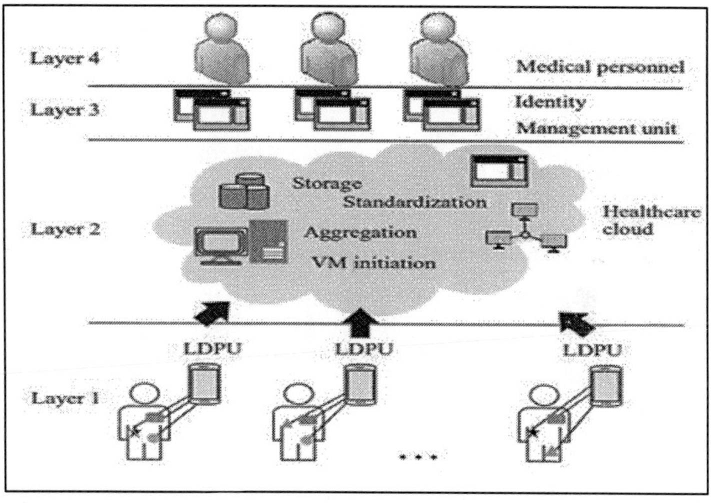

Fig. 4.5 AmbuSens Architecture

Communication Module

Each sensor node is equipped with a Bluetooth module that follows the IEEE 802.15.1 standard. This module enables short-range communication—up to 10 meters in clear line-of-sight—between the sensor nodes and the Local Data Processing Unit (LDPU). After collecting data from the sensors, the LDPU forwards it to the cloud using mobile networks such as 3G or 4G, ensuring reliable and continuous data transfer.

4.3 Agriculture IoT – Introduction and Case Studies

1. Introduction to Agriculture IoT

Agriculture IoT refers to the integration of **smart sensors, communication networks, cloud computing, and automation technologies** into farming activities. The goal is to **increase productivity, reduce manual effort, improve resource management, and enable data-driven decisions**.

In this system, sensors installed in fields continuously collect data such as:

- Soil moisture
- Temperature and humidity
- Light intensity
- Crop growth parameters
- Water level
- Pest activity

This data is sent to the cloud using technologies like **Wi-Fi, LoRaWAN, GSM/4G/5G, or Bluetooth**, where it is analyzed. Based on the analysis, farmers can take informed actions or even automate tasks like irrigation and fertilization.

Key Features of Agriculture IoT

- **Real-time monitoring:** Track field conditions anytime.
- **Precision agriculture:** Apply water, fertilizer, or pesticides only where needed.
- **Automation:** Automatic irrigation and greenhouse control.
- **Data analytics:** Predict crop growth, weather patterns, and soil behavior.
- **Resource efficiency:** Saves water, energy, and fertilizers.

Benefits

- Higher crop yield
- Reduced labor costs
- Prevents crop damage through early alerts
- Improves product quality
- Enhances sustainable farming practices

2. Components of Agriculture IoT System

a) Sensors

- **Soil moisture sensor** – measures water content
- **DHT11/DHT22** – temperature & humidity
- **LDR** – sunlight availability
- **pH sensor** – soil acidity
- **CO_2 / gas sensor** – greenhouse environment monitoring

b) Communication Technologies

- Wi-Fi
- LoRaWAN
- ZigBee
- GSM/4G/5G
- Bluetooth

c) Controllers

- Arduino
- Raspberry Pi
- ESP32

d) Cloud Platforms

- AWS IoT
- Google Firebase
- ThingsBoard
- Azure IoT

e) Actuators

- Motors for irrigation
- Sprinklers
- Fertilizer dispensers

- Fans and heaters in greenhouses

3. Case Studies of Agriculture IoT

Case Study 1: Smart Irrigation System

Overview

A smart irrigation system automates watering based on soil moisture readings. Instead of irrigating on fixed intervals, the pump runs only when the soil becomes dry.

How It Works

1. Soil moisture sensor reads real-time soil water levels.
2. Sensor data is sent to a microcontroller (ESP32/Arduino).
3. If moisture is below the threshold, the controller activates the water pump through a relay.
4. Farmers receive notifications on a mobile app or dashboard.
5. Data is stored in cloud for tracking seasonal changes.

Impact

- Up to **40–60% water savings**
- Crop health improves due to optimal watering
- Reduces labor and prevents over-irrigation

Case Study 2: Smart Greenhouse Monitoring

Overview

Greenhouses require controlled environmental conditions for sensitive crops. IoT helps monitor and automatically adjust these conditions.

Technologies Used

- Temperature & humidity sensors (DHT22)
- Light sensors (LDR)
- Soil sensors
- Actuators: fans, heaters, sprinklers
- Wi-Fi or ZigBee network

How It Works

1. Sensors monitor climate parameters inside the greenhouse.

2. Data is analyzed by a controller (ESP32/Raspberry Pi).
3. If temperature is high → fans turn on.
4. If humidity is low → misting system activates.
5. If sunlight is insufficient → artificial lights turn on.
6. Farmer checks the live dashboard remotely.

Impact

- Stable climate → higher yield
- Reduced crop failure
- Energy-efficient resource management

Case Study 3: Smart Crop Disease Detection

Overview

IoT devices combined with AI and imaging techniques can identify early signs of crop diseases.

How It Works

1. Cameras capture images of crop leaves.
2. Images are processed through AI models (CNN-based).
3. Algorithm identifies symptoms like spots, discoloration, fungus, etc.
4. Alerts are sent to farmers with recommended treatment.
5. Data is stored to track disease spread patterns.

Impact

- Early diagnosis → prevents large-scale infection
- Reduces need for heavy pesticide use
- Cost savings & healthier crops

Case Study 4: Livestock Monitoring System

Overview

IoT devices placed on animals help monitor their health, movements, and environmental conditions.

Technologies Used

- GPS modules
- Temperature sensors

- Heart-rate sensors
- LoRaWAN/GSM communication

How It Works

1. Devices track the location, body temperature, and activity of cattle.
2. Anomalies like fever or abnormal movement trigger alerts.
3. Farmers receive data on their phones.
4. Helps detect diseases like mastitis early.

Impact

- Better livestock health management
- Prevents animal loss and theft
- Improves milk and meat productivity

4.4 IoT Analytics -Introduction

Overview of Machine Learning

The term *machine learning* was first introduced in 1959 by Arthur Lee Samuel. He described it as a field that enables computers to improve their performance by learning from experience rather than relying solely on explicit programming. Machine Learning combines principles from statistics, mathematics, and computer science to analyze data, build models, and create systems capable of autonomous decision-making.

Advantages of Machine Learning

Machine Learning offers several powerful benefits that make it essential in modern applications:

Major Advantages

- **Task Automation:** ML systems can take over repetitive, routine, or time-consuming tasks, reducing manual effort and minimizing errors.
- **High Accuracy:** By analyzing large volumes of data, ML models can generate precise predictions and insights, often outperforming traditional methods.
- **Insight Discovery:** ML algorithms uncover hidden trends, correlations, and anomalies within datasets that may not be visible to analysts.

- **Personalized Experiences:** Businesses use ML to tailor recommendations, marketing content, and user interactions based on individual behavior.
- **Scalability:** ML models can process and adapt to extremely large datasets without compromising speed or performance.
- **Self-Improvement:** As more data becomes available, ML models refine their knowledge and continuously enhance their performance.
- **Predictive Power:** Organizations leverage ML for forecasting customer behavior, market trends, risks, and operational demands.
- **Cost Efficiency:** Automation and optimization reduce long-term operational expenses.
- **Better Security:** ML helps detect suspicious activities, fraud, or system anomalies in real time, strengthening cybersecurity.

Challenges in Machine Learning

Although Machine Learning drives innovation across industries, developing reliable ML solutions is challenging. Experts must deal with inconsistent data, changing environments, model biases, and complex deployment issues. Below are the major challenges faced in ML:

1. Data Quality and Availability

ML models rely completely on the data they are trained on. However, real-world data is usually incomplete, noisy, or unorganized. Professionals often spend most of their time cleaning and preparing data. Obtaining high-quality, labeled datasets—especially in fields like healthcare—is expensive and requires significant effort.

Example: In healthcare systems, missing or inconsistent patient information can lead to inaccurate predictions or diagnoses.

2. Imbalanced Datasets

Some datasets contain very few examples of critical classes. When one class dominates, models become biased and ignore minority cases.

Example: Fraudulent transactions make up less than 1% of financial data but failing to detect them can cause major monetary losses.

3. Overfitting and Underfitting

- **Overfitting:** The model memorizes noise instead of patterns.
- **Underfitting:** The model is too simple and misses important relationships.

Striking a balance and ensuring good generalization is one of the biggest challenges in ML.

Example: A stock prediction model might work well on past data but fail when new market conditions arise.

4. Lack of Interpretability

Many modern ML models—particularly deep networks—act like black boxes. They provide outputs without clear reasoning, making it hard to justify decisions or comply with regulations.

Example: A loan system denying applications without explanation creates trust and legal issues.

5. Model Deployment and Integration Issues

Moving a trained model into a real-world environment requires integration with databases, APIs, and live systems. Technical mismatches often prevent successful deployment.

Example: A recommendation model may crash when exposed to heavy real-time user traffic.

6. Model Drift and Performance Degradation

As real-world data changes over time, model accuracy decreases. This gradual decline—called model drift—requires continuous monitoring and retraining.

Example: A churn prediction model based on last year's customer behavior becomes inaccurate as trends evolve.

7. Data Privacy and Security Risks

ML systems frequently use sensitive information. Ensuring user privacy, preventing data leakage, and complying with laws like GDPR and HIPAA are major challenges.

Example: Training deep learning models on medical images without proper anonymization can violate privacy rules.

8. Bias and Fairness Issues

Bias can enter a model from skewed data, poor feature selection, or historical inequalities. This results in unfair outcomes.

Example: A facial recognition system may misidentify people from specific demographic groups more often.

9. Lack of Domain Knowledge

ML engineers must understand the domain to interpret results correctly. Without subject expertise, even accurate models may lead to wrong conclusions.

Example: A financial model built without economic understanding may fail to consider market cycles.

10. Rapid Technological Advancements and Skill Gaps

The ML field evolves quickly. New algorithms, frameworks, and tools appear faster than professionals can learn them, creating skill shortages.

Example: Engineers familiar with earlier ML workflows may struggle with advanced methods like MLOps or transformer-based models.

Types of Machine Learning

Machine Learning (ML) is an important area of Artificial Intelligence (AI) that focuses on creating models and algorithms capable of learning from data. Instead of being programmed with fixed instructions, ML systems identify patterns, improve through experience, and make decisions much like humans do. By analyzing past data and recognizing relationships, these systems can generate predictions, classifications, and insights without manual intervention.

Machine Learning techniques are grouped into several categories based on how they learn from data. The major types of ML are:

- **Supervised Machine Learning**
- **Unsupervised Machine Learning**
- **Reinforcement Learning**

Along with these, two additional learning approaches are often used:

- **Semi-Supervised Learning**
- **Self-Supervised Learning**

These combine characteristics of both supervised and unsupervised learning.

1. Supervised Machine Learning

Supervised learning is a technique in which the model is trained using a **labeled dataset**. A labeled dataset means that every input is paired with the correct output (known as the label).

The model studies this relationship during training and learns how to predict the correct output for new data.

Key Characteristics

- Uses labeled data containing both inputs and outputs
- Learns a mapping between features (inputs) and target values (outputs)
- Involves two main sets of data:
  - **Training dataset** – used to teach the model
  - **Validation/testing dataset** – used to evaluate the model's accuracy
- Produces highly reliable results when data is clean and properly labeled

Examples

- Predicting house prices
- Classifying emails as spam or not spam
- Diagnosing diseases based on medical test results

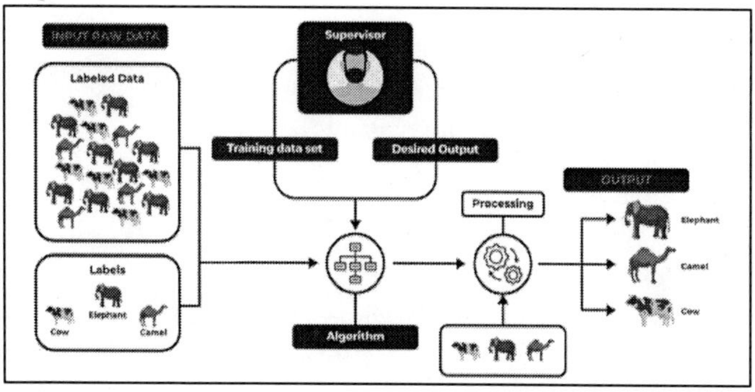

Fig. 4.6 Supervised Learning

Example:

When a model is trained using labeled pictures of cats and dogs, it observes the unique features of each category. Later, when a new image is provided, the model uses what it learned to identify whether the image belongs to a cat or a dog.

Supervised learning is broadly divided into two major types:

1. Classification

Classification deals with predicting **categorical outputs**, such as assigning inputs to predefined groups or classes. For example, determining whether an email is *spam or not spam*, or identifying whether a tumor is *benign or malignant*.

In classification, the algorithm learns the relationship between input features and class labels and then uses this knowledge to classify new data.

Popular Classification Algorithms

- Logistic Regression
- Decision Tree
- Random Forest
- K-Nearest Neighbors (KNN)
- Naive Bayes
- Support Vector Machine (SVM)

2. Regression

Regression focuses on predicting **continuous values**, meaning numerical outputs.

Common examples include forecasting house prices, estimating sales, or predicting temperature.

These algorithms learn the mathematical relationship between input variables and a continuous target value.

Widely Used Regression Algorithms

- Linear Regression
- Polynomial Regression
- Ridge Regression
- Lasso Regression
- Decision Tree Regression
- Random Forest Regression

Use Cases of Supervised Learning

Supervised learning is ideal in situations where:

- Labeled data is available.
- The goal is to predict a category or a value.
- Historical datasets already contain the correct outputs.

Applications of Supervised Learning

Supervised ML is used across numerous real-world fields, such as:

1. Image, Speech, and Text Processing

- Image recognition (e.g., identifying objects in photos)
- Speech-to-text conversion
- Sentiment analysis of customer reviews

2. Predictive Analytics

- Sales forecasting
- Customer churn prediction
- Stock market trend prediction
- Weather forecasting

3. Personalization and Recommendations

- Product recommendations on e-commerce websites

- Movie suggestions on streaming platforms

4. Healthcare and Finance

- Disease identification
- Credit scoring
- Fraud detection

5. Automation and Control Systems

- Quality checks in manufacturing
- Autonomous driving
- Smart gaming systems

2. Unsupervised Machine Learning

Unsupervised learning works with **data that has no labels**, meaning the system is not told what the correct output should be. Instead, the algorithm studies the data on its own, discovers hidden structures, groups similar items, and identifies meaningful patterns.

This type of learning is especially useful for:

- Clustering similar objects
- Reducing the dimensionality of data
- Visualizing complex datasets

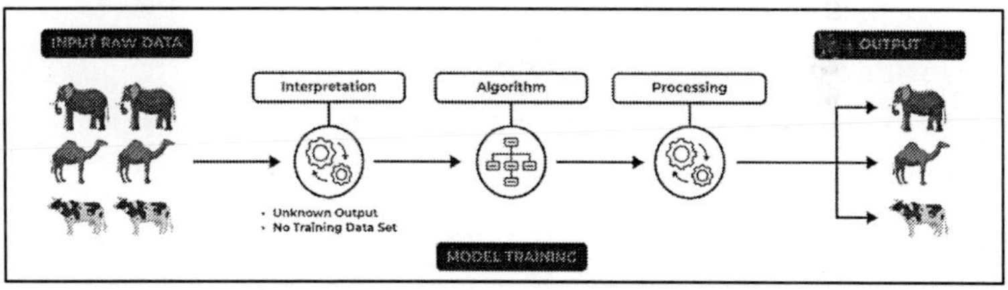

Fig. 4.7 Unsupervised Learning

Example:

Suppose you have a collection of customer data but no labels. An unsupervised learning algorithm can automatically group customers based on their buying habits. These groups, or clusters, are extremely valuable for marketing, customer segmentation, and targeted campaigns.

Unsupervised learning is mainly divided into the following categories:

1. Clustering

Clustering involves organizing data into groups where items within the same group share similar characteristics.

It helps uncover hidden structures without relying on labeled training data.

Popular Clustering Techniques

- **K-Means Clustering**
- **DBSCAN (Density-Based Spatial Clustering of Applications with Noise)**
- **Mean-Shift Clustering**

These techniques are commonly used in customer grouping, image segmentation, and pattern detection.

2. Dimensionality Reduction

Dimensionality reduction simplifies a dataset by decreasing the number of features while keeping essential information intact.

It is very useful for speeding up models, visualizing complex data, and removing noise.

Common Dimensionality Reduction Methods

- **Principal Component Analysis (PCA)**
- **Independent Component Analysis (ICA)**

These methods are widely applied in image compression, bioinformatics, and feature extraction.

3. Association Rule Learning

Association rule learning identifies meaningful relationships between items in large datasets.

It finds rules that show how the presence of one item influences the likelihood of another appearing.

Common Association Rule Algorithms

- **Apriori**
- **FP-Growth**
- **Eclat**

This technique is frequently used in market basket analysis—for example, identifying that customers who buy bread often buy butter.

Applications of Unsupervised Learning

Unsupervised learning is suitable when:

- The data has no labels or predefined categories
- You want to explore hidden patterns in data
- You need clustering, grouping, or feature extraction

It's commonly applied in:

- Marketing and customer segmentation
- Fraud and anomaly detection
- Recommender systems
- Exploratory data analysis

Applications of Unsupervised Learning

Some major real-world uses include:

- **Clustering & Segmentation:** Grouping customers, documents, or images
- **Anomaly Detection:** Identifying unusual behavior or outliers
- **Dimensionality Reduction:** Simplifying large datasets for faster processing
- **Marketing & Recommendations:** Understanding customer preferences and behavior
- **Data Preprocessing:** Cleaning data, extracting features, and discovering patterns

Reinforcement Learning

Reinforcement Learning (RL) is a learning approach where an **agent** improves its performance through interaction with an **environment**. Instead of learning from labeled examples, the agent learns by performing actions and receiving feedback in the form of **rewards or penalties**.

Over time, the agent figures out which actions lead to better results and gradually develops an optimal strategy.

Key Idea

- The agent takes an action
- The environment responds with a reward or punishment
- Based on this feedback, the agent updates its behavior
- Eventually, it discovers the best sequence of actions to maximize total rewards

Reinforcement learning is widely used in:

- Robotics and autonomous systems
- Gaming AI (e.g., AlphaGo, chess engines, self-learning bots)
- Recommendation systems
- Industrial automation
- Navigation and path optimization

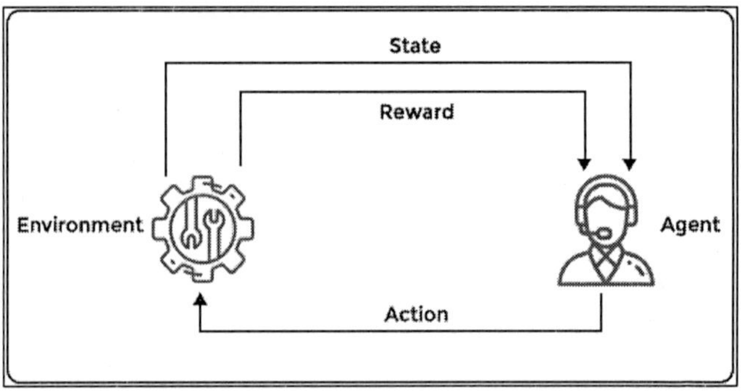

Fig. 4.8 Reinforcement Machine Learning

Example

Imagine an AI system learning to play chess. It receives **positive feedback** when it makes strong moves and **negative feedback** for weak ones. By continuously interacting with the game, the agent gradually discovers strategies that increase its chances of winning.

Popular Reinforcement Learning Algorithms

- **Q-Learning:** This algorithm finds the optimal action for every state by estimating the expected long-term rewards.
- **SARSA (State–Action–Reward–State–Action):** Works like Q-

Learning but updates its values based on the actual action taken, making it more conservative.

- **Deep Q-Learning (DQN):** Uses deep neural networks to manage complex or high-dimensional state spaces, making it suitable for advanced RL tasks.

Types of Reinforcement Learning

- **Positive Reinforcement:** Increases the likelihood of a behavior by rewarding correct or desirable actions *Example: awarding points for correct answers.*
- **Negative Reinforcement:** Encourages better behavior by removing an unpleasant outcome *Example: disabling a warning sound once the right move is made.*

Scenarios Suitable for Applying Reinforcement Learning:

- The system must learn by **interacting directly with its environment**.
- The task involves **decision-making, optimization, or a series of actions**.
- Long-term results and adaptive behavior matter more than short-term accuracy.
- The solution requires continuous improvement from trial-and-error feedback.

Applications of Reinforcement Learning

Reinforcement learning is widely used in areas such as:

- **Games and simulations** – training intelligent players or NPCs.
- **Robotics** – enabling robots to adapt and perform tasks autonomously.
- **Self-driving vehicles** – supporting real-time decision-making.
- **Healthcare and finance** – for treatment optimization, trading, and resource planning.
- **Recommendation systems** – providing personalized and evolving suggestions.

- **Industrial control & energy management** – improving efficiency and system performance.

Semi-Supervised Learning (Combination of Supervised & Unsupervised Learning)

Semi-Supervised Learning is an approach that blends **labeled** and **unlabeled** data. A small portion of labeled data guides the learning process, while the large amount of unlabeled data helps the model understand patterns and structure. This technique is especially valuable when labeling data is expensive, time-consuming, or requires expert knowledge.

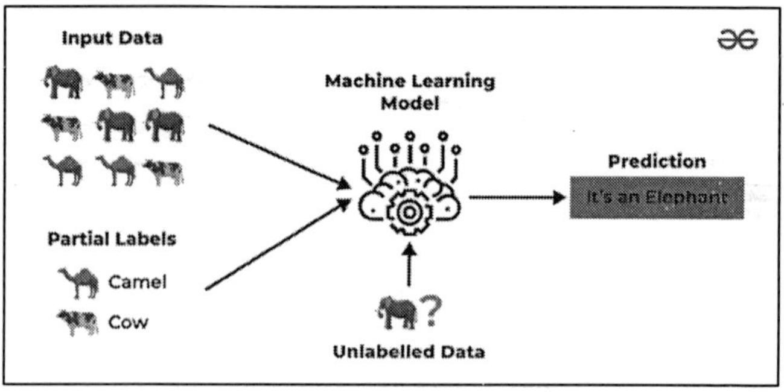

Fig. 4.9 Semi-Supervised Learning

Example

Imagine developing a language translation system. Getting labeled translations for every sentence pair is costly and time-consuming. Semi-supervised learning helps by using a small set of labeled sentence pairs along with a large number of unlabeled sentences. This combination allows the model to learn patterns more effectively, resulting in better translation quality. Many modern machine translation tools have improved significantly using this approach.

Situations Suitable for Semi-Supervised Learning

- When labeled data is scarce, but there is plenty of unlabeled data available.
- When labeling requires domain expertise, such as in medical imaging, natural language processing, or complex visual datasets.
- When the unlabeled data contains valuable patterns that can boost model accuracy.

Applications of Semi-Supervised Learning

- **Image Classification:** Improves performance by combining a small set of labeled images with a much larger pool of unlabeled ones.
- **Natural Language Processing:** Enhances language models by training on limited annotated text along with vast unlabeled corpora.
- **Speech Recognition:** Achieves higher accuracy by using limited transcribed audio plus large amounts of raw speech data.
- **Recommendation Systems:** Utilizes sparse labeled data with abundant user interaction logs to generate better recommendations.
- **Healthcare & Medical Imaging:** Supports diagnosis by analyzing both annotated and unannotated medical scans.

Self-Supervised Learning

Self-Supervised Learning (SSL) is an advanced technique where models create their own labels directly from raw data. Instead of depending on manual annotation, the model trains itself by predicting one part of the data using another part.

Example of Self-Supervised Learning

In Natural Language Processing, models like **BERT** or **GPT** learn by predicting missing or masked words within a sentence. By understanding the context around the masked word, the model develops strong language comprehension—without needing human-labeled data.

Popular Self-Supervised Techniques

- **Masked Language Modeling (e.g., BERT)**
- **Contrastive Learning** (SimCLR, MoCo)

- **Autoencoders** (learning to reconstruct input data)
- **Predictive Coding** (predicting future or missing representations)

Applications of Self-Supervised Learning

Self-supervised learning is widely used in:

- **Natural Language Processing** – for building strong language representations.
- **Computer Vision and Speech Recognition** – using unlabeled images or audio.
- **Video Understanding** – recognizing actions or events across frames.
- **Pre-training Large AI Models** – foundation models are often trained using SSL before fine-tuning.

Optimal Applications of Self-Supervised Learning

- Obtaining labeled data is difficult, expensive, or impractical.
- Working with large datasets like images, audio recordings, or huge text collections.
- You need strong pre-trained models that can later be adapted to specific supervised tasks.

Comparison of various ML related Techniques

Table 4.6

Type	Data Requirement	Label Availability	Learning Goal	Common Use Case
Supervised	High	Labeled	Predict outputs	Spam detection, Price prediction
Unsupervised	Medium	Unlabeled	Find hidden patterns	Customer segmentation

Reinforcement	High	Reward feedback	Learn best actions	Robotics, Games
Semi-Supervised	Medium	Partial labels	Combine both learning types	NLP, Image recognition
Self-Supervised	High	Self-generated labels	Learn data representations	BERT, GPT, CLIP

Exercise

MCQs (Multiple Choice Questions)

1 Agricultural IoT mainly helps in:

a) Entertainment

b) Crop monitoring and precision farming

c) Vehicle tracking

d) Patient monitoring

Answer: b) Crop monitoring and precision farming

2 Which of the following is a common IoT application in vehicular systems?

a) Soil moisture sensing

b) Traffic management and vehicle tracking

c) Heart rate monitoring

d) Cloud storage

Answer: b) Traffic management and vehicle tracking

3 Healthcare IoT primarily focuses on:

a) Crop irrigation

b) Real-time patient monitoring and telemedicine

c) Fleet management

d) Industrial automation

Answer: b) Real-time patient monitoring and telemedicine

4 IoT analytics helps organizations to:

a) Store data only

b) Extract insights from IoT-generated data

c) Manufacture IoT devices

d) Reduce sensor count

Answer: b) Extract insights from IoT-generated data

5 A typical example of Agricultural IoT is:

a) Smart irrigation system

b) GPS vehicle navigation

c) Smart hospital beds

d) Social media analytics

Answer: a) Smart irrigation system

Very Short Answer Questions

1. Define Agricultural IoT.
2. Mention one key application of Vehicular IoT.
3. What is the main focus of Healthcare IoT?
4. Define IoT Analytics in one sentence.
5. Give one example of an IoT-based smart farming solution.

Short Answer Questions

1. Explain the role of IoT in modern agriculture with an example.
2. How does Vehicular IoT improve traffic safety and management?
3. Discuss two real-world applications of Healthcare IoT.
4. What is IoT Analytics, and why is it important for decision-making?
5. Describe how IoT helps in precision farming.

Long Answer Questions

1. Discuss Agricultural IoT, including its key applications, benefits, and a brief case study.

2. Explain Vehicular IoT, highlighting its technologies, applications, and impact on transportation systems.

3. Describe Healthcare IoT, including examples of case studies, patient monitoring systems, and telemedicine applications.

4. Explain the concept of IoT Analytics, its workflow, and how it supports intelligent decision-making in IoT ecosystems.

5. Compare and contrast Agricultural, Vehicular, and Healthcare IoT in terms of applications, challenges, and societal impact.